Thank you for your generosity & for always being so amazing at nurturing the feel of part of the family! I look forward to celebrating & continuing to grow (as I know we will become good friends as well as family)!

All my love!

P.S. I hope you love this image as much as I do! We should investigate our love for detail!

JULIA!!!

Thank you for your never ending generosity, & for always being so amazing at making me feel apart of the family! I look forward at our reletionship continuing to grow as it has, I know we will become good friends as well as family!

All my love!

[signature] x

p.s. I hope you love the images in this book! You have such an incredible eye for detail!

KITCHEN COCKTAILS
RECIPES OF

THE LONDON COCKTAIL CLUB

BY
JJ GOODMAN

"We opened The London Cocktail Club in 2008 with the intention of creating a bartender's paradise! A bar that parties like the best of them, and mixes the world's greatest drinks to perfection. A place where you can dance on the tables whilst singing to AC/DC, sipping on the perfect dry Martini!"

J.J. GOODMAN
BARTENDER

First published in Great Britain in 2018 on behalf of:
The London Cocktail Club, Arch 253, Paradise Row, Bethnal Green,
London, E2 9LE
Tel: +44(0)20 7580 1960
Email: info@londoncocktailclub.co.uk
www.londoncocktailclub.co.uk

Published by:
RMC Media - www.rmcmedia.co.uk
6 Broadfield Court, Sheffield, S8 0XF
Tel: 0114 250 6300

Text and design © RMC Media, 2018
Photography © Jodi Hinds (www.jodihinds.com) 2018

Author: JJ Goodman, with James Coston, Robb Collins, Martin Edwards and Jo Davison
Design: Richard Abbey
Front Cover Design: Marc Ross, Dirty Hands Co. 5th Floor, Carliol Square, Newcastle upon Tyne, NE1 6UF
dirtyhandsco.com
Proof-reader: Christopher Brierley

The moral right of the author has been asserted. All rights reserved. No part of this publication may be reproduced, stored in a retrieval system or transmitted in any form or by any means, electronic, mechanical, photocopying, recording or otherwise, without the prior written consent of the copyright owners.

Printed and bound in Malta by:
Gutenberg Press Ltd - www.gutenberg.com.mt
Gudja Road, Tarxien, Malta, GXQ 2902
Tel: 00356 2189 7037

A CIP catalogue record for this book is available from the British Library.

ISBN: 978-1-907998-32-4

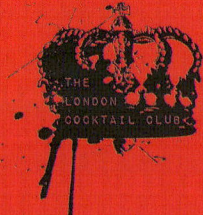 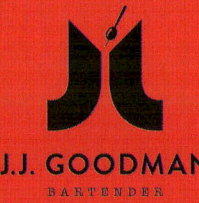 

PRICE: £30

Welcome to my 24 hours of cocktail culture!

Each chapter takes you through my favourite cocktails, from dusk till dawn and beyond! I'm often asked "what's your favourite cocktail?" and my answer is simple. It depends on the country I'm in, the weather outside, and the time of day!

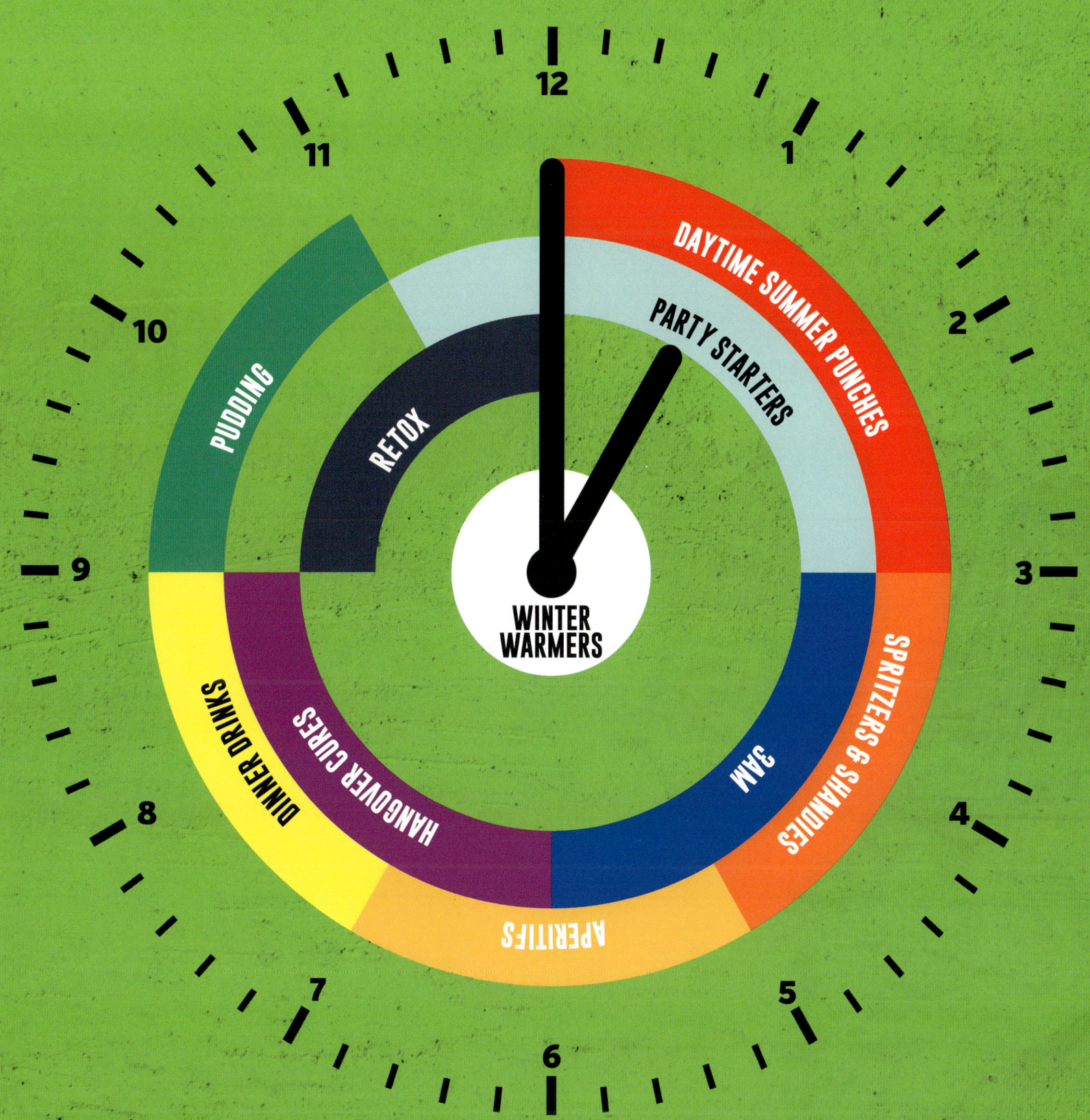

8	**DEDICATIONS**
12	**FOREWORDS** RAYMOND BLANC OBE / SARAH WILLINGHAM
14	**WELCOME TO THE LONDON COCKTAIL CLUB**
17	**JJ GOODMAN**
18	**MASTER OF MIXOLOGY**

- 18 WELCOME TO THE CLASS
- 20 THEORY OF MIXOLOGY
- 21 TOOLS OF THE TRADE
- 22 THE LANGUAGE OF COCKTAILS
- 28 MAKING THE BASICS
- 29 GLASSWARE
- 30 THE BARTENDER'S DOZEN
- 35 THE TEN COMMANDMENTS

***

38	**DAYTIME SUMMER PUNCHES**
56	**SPRITZERS & SHANDIES**

74	**APERITIFS**
92	**DINNER DRINKS**
110	**PUDDING**
128	**PARTY STARTERS**
146	**3AM**
164	**HANGOVER CURES**
182	**RETOX**
200	**WINTER WARMERS**

***

218	**RAYMOND BLANC** *CHEESE FONDUE*
222	**INDEX**
224	**JJ'S RECOMMENDED READS**

Big thanks to ALL the team who made this book happen! Martin Edwards at RMC Media, Richard Abbey on design, my LCC family, Jodi Hinds our incredible photographer, Ryan Baker who never stopped pushing, Jesper Lundin my master mixologist, Robb Collins who brought our stories to life, and James Coston for being my wingman throughout, thank you all, this book is as much yours as it is mine!

Before we get going in this book I need to show some love for some truly special people in my life, because without them I wouldn't be where I am today.

Ben McCreanor for igniting my love of bartending, Frosty for teaching me the foundations for success, Lee Lynch for being the consummate professional, Tim Bacon for proving anything is possible, Leigh Miller for inspiring me to always work harder, Ben Martin for pushing me further than I thought I could go, Tim Oakley for unlocking my creativity for mixology, Lance Perkins for giving me the freedom to realise my potential, Lee Ottery for being my number one soldier, Sean Ware for stretching the limitations of my imagination, Raymond Blanc for showing me that dedication mixed with creativity can take you anywhere, Sarah Willingham for always watching over me, I owe you so much, James Hopkins for always being there when I need you most, big love brother!

Finally nothing would be possible without my mum Lizzie, who taught me "no fear, no greed". I haven't, I'm not, I never will. I love you, thank you for always inspiring me to follow my dreams.

FOREWORDS

Raymond Blanc OBE

It is now seven years since I first worked with JJ and James. I'm proud to be associated with such an exciting venture - brimming with ideas, developing their creativity and mentoring the two wonderful people who are at the heart of this success. And, as the story unfolds, JJ and James are passing-on their skills to the very strong team around them. Together, they have made the London Cocktail Club one of the most creative places to meet, have fun and, of course, enjoy a cocktail. My personal favourite is the Rose Petal Martini (page 80). Oh, and one cannot forget the Paloma (page 84). Anyone who knows me knows my affection for the fragrant purple flower.

I first met JJ and James in 2009 when they were contestants on a TV programme I was making for the BBC: The Restaurant, Series 3. The concept of the show was for me to challenge, and then invest in, the most talented duo from nine pairs of aspiring restaurateurs. These two young men were by no means the best chefs I've ever seen, and to add insult to injury, JJ began winking at me each time he saw me! I promised myself that I would get my revenge on his cheeky attitude. I'd never have guessed then, that this same cheeky chap I'd grow to love.

As the show unfolded, it became obvious all of the contestants were rookies and would ruin me if I went into business with them. After an emergency meeting with my fellow judges on the show - Sarah Willingham and David Moore - we scoured through all their applications to find inspiration... And then I found my gold! I was thrilled to find that JJ had just won the Cocktail World Cup! So, he wasn't the best cook... but my God he could make cocktails! JJ and James went on to win the show and, together with my fellow judges, instead of challenging them to create a restaurant we challenged them to create a cocktail bar of which we all became directors.

This is JJ's first book and I am extremely proud, as a friend and mentor, to see his success. He himself has become a mentor now too - providing opportunities for Britain's unemployed youth. He's even creating the first government-accredited qualification in cocktail bartending. What a fantastic initiative.

And of course, being a chef, I could not help it: I have snuck a little recipe into this book from my home to yours... something warming and indulgent to accompany all the inspired cocktails you'll now be able to make yourself.

Bravo, JJ!

Sarah Willingham

Anyone who knows JJ knows that if he was ever going to write a book.. this was always going to be it! The London Cocktail Club (LCC) was built on his passion to make exceptional cocktails available to anyone, this just takes it one step further… into our homes. Come to an LCC and anyone is welcome, just like anyone can make the best cocktails in the world at home from ingredients that you can buy at any supermarket.

This is SO JJ! No cloak and mirrors, no 'ponce', he is keeping it simple, making his incredible talent and himself accessible and passing on his creativity to anyone who wants to learn.

Every business needs some 'magic' and JJ is ours. He's just got it! The key to the success in this business is to build foundations and operate a strong, solid business AROUND this magic to allow it to flourish. The team at LCC are some of the best people I've ever met in the industry and provide the incredible structure that hones JJ's ethos. One of the things we're so proud of is that they learn their trade, find their own magic and so many go off and do their own thing. Attracting the best in the industry is testimony to JJ's brilliance.

When I first met JJ, on BBC's The Restaurant, he was wide-eyed and FULL of passion and drive. He not only had an extraordinary talent but he respected that in order to have a successful business 'magic' isn't enough. Enter James, his best mate and business partner over the years. The two of them together are unstoppable and have not only built a phenomenal business together but remained best friends throughout. I am so proud to share their journey and to call them both very close friends.

The London Cocktail Club was my first TV investment and I couldn't be prouder. The business flourishes and we continue to expand and hire fantastic people to help us do this. The business model is the best I've ever seen in the industry and we continue to open sites that beat all of our expectations. Seeing London Cocktail Club move outside of London is a big moment for us all. I hope I'm in business with the boys for many, many years to come.

This book is a MUST-have for anyone's coffee table. I hope you all enjoy it as much as I have.

An audience of millions watched young bartender JJ Goodman and his best mate James 'Hoppy' Hopkins shoot to fame as winners of a reality TV show in 2009.

Viewers of BBC2's The Restaurant, starring Raymond Blanc OBE and Dragon's Den star panellist Sarah Willingham, warmed to their effervescent enthusiasm and the way every challenge they were set left the 25-year-old pals stirred, but never shaken.

JJ and James had no training as chefs, but had already proved they had the recipe for success having opened their own cocktail club in Covent Garden six months before. And their prize, a business partnership with Blanc and Willingham, enabled them to launch a new venture, The London Cocktail Club.

Today the LCC is now a ten-strong institution on the capital's night scene, a brand credited with sparking the cocktail revolution now sweeping the UK.

Customers adore the LCC's eclectic and unpretentious surroundings, where they are served innovative creations by some of the world's most skilled bartenders and glowing reviews have been penned by numerous respected publications - from Time Out, Design My Night and View London to World's Best Bars.

And the one ingredient the LCC could not be without is JJ Goodman.

A maverick mixer and pioneering trend-setter, his creations have shaken up the cocktail as we thought we knew it. He deliberately breaks the rules and re-invents, whipping up concoctions with the zeal of the archetypal mad professor. Bacon & Egg Martini anyone? Or perhaps a deep, dark Squid Ink Sour will float your boat?

Pick up your glass, clink and trust - because each and every seemingly outlandish concoction has been painstakingly balanced. After all, JJ's flavour-pairing skills WERE picked up at the feet of his Michelin Star mentor, Blanc.

Small wonder accolade after industry accolade have come JJ's way. He's been named in London Lifestyle Award's 50 Most Influential People and Zagat's Trailblazers under 30, won The London Bar and Club Awards and the 42 Below Cocktail World Cup. His creative skills are in big demand from some of the world's biggest brands - he's even worked at Buckingham Palace.

But the mixology maverick is not done yet… His next mission? To demystify the cocktail-making process and share the secrets and short-cuts that enable every novice to get in the mix.

Ladies and gentlemen, reach for your shaker, fill the ice-maker - and prepare to get your London Cocktail Club House Party freak on…

AWARDS & NOMINATIONS:

Gold medallist at the 42 Below Cocktail World Cup 2008

Opened the first London Cocktail Club 2008

BBC2's 'The Restaurant' Winner 2009

London Lifestyle awards '50 Most Influential'

Zagat's 30 under 30 trailblazers

Tales of the Cocktail Finalist for - "Best International High Volume Cocktail Bar" 2015

Harpers 'Top 20' Most Influential in the UK Bar Industry 2018

IMBIBE Chairman's Award 2018

Springboard Award for Best Employer and Best Career Progression 2018

DEDICATIONS

I'm proud as punch to have finally gotten the chance to write my first book, with chapters that take you through 24 hours of my cocktail world, and drinks that I truly love!

The cocktail revolution has to start at home, which is why my "Kitchen Cocktails" book was conceived. Discover all of my favourite classic cocktails, blended with my very own original recipes, some of which you will have sampled over the last decade at one of my London Cocktail Clubs.

Here you'll find all my favourite recipes are mixed ONLY using ingredients found in the supermarket, so anyone can grab what they need with ease and start shaking straight away.

No more expensive lacquers and spirits that you only use once, that then collect dust in your cupboard, and most importantly, waste money. With this book, I will strip away the mythology behind "complicated" cocktails, teach you the short-cuts, tips and secrets that professional bartenders use to make perfect-tasting drinks every time, without breaking your back.

I've given a nod on every page to the fascinating histories behind each drink, and even the recipes for the hardcore purists to follow. But if you, like me, want super tasty drinks, quickly and cheaply at home without hassle, then this is the cocktail bible for you.

I've taken those same legendary drinks and remade them to be simple, easy, and in most cases, tastier than their forefathers. I'd love this book to be your trusted go-to guide for a fun night in with friends, not something you leaf through and stick on a shelf forever more.

You'll probably make a few mistakes as you're starting out, but I promise you, the more you make the better you will become. Keep mixing - and have fun!

JJ Goodman

MASTER OF MIXOLOGY

WELCOME TO THE CLASS

Back in the eighties and nineties it was cool to be a Master of the Universe. But times change. Why settle for second best when you too can become a Master of Mixology? All you need is the know-how.

The London Cocktail Club has that by the bucketload and we don't want to keep it all to ourselves.

Through the pages of this book, which we hope becomes your cocktail bible, we will be your personal mixology tutors.

The secret methods and little tips we've learned from some of the world's most talented bartenders will be revealed - along with many more we've invented all by ourselves.

Why? Because we are generous souls. And we want to stir up a home cocktail-making revolution.

Comrades, to arms! No longer will there be ingredients that are hard to find and which seem an expensive outlay for the amount involved. And the recipes? Down with the old order! No more shall you fear recipes that seem so complicated that you wouldn't dare try them out. You won't find any fancy crushed ice in here, only good old party bag ice, we have even been mixing our Margaritas with pasteurised citrus juice so no more hand squeezing your citrus if you can't be bothered; you're welcome folks!

So let's demystify the art of mixology and prove to you that cocktails CAN be easy and cheap to make. And they're a fun alternative to drinking beer and wine at home.

Turn the pages for a lesson in the basic techniques, the preferred ingredients and go-to equipment beloved by the best bartenders. Find out what ingredients go together and the theories and rules the experts use to create their own, unique cocktails.

But just as importantly, discover that making cocktails is easy and affordable, and that putting your own spin on recipes is fun and creative.

You will also get an idea of how little it actually costs to make great cocktails.

Welcome to the LCC Masters of Mixology Programme. Roll up your sleeves and get ready to learn…

THEORY OF MIXOLOGY

Once you learn the structure of how drinks are made, understanding mixology becomes very simple. Each style of drink is made from a pretty basic recipe. The trick is to get inventive with different flavours, vessels, garnishes and aromas... That's what it's all about.

Let's start with the basic formula for success. Stick to this and you can't go wrong:

Collins Formula:

1 part sour (25ml) • *Your sour element is citrus (lime, lemon, grapefruit, orange etc)*
1 part sweet (25ml) • *Your sweet element can be sugar syrup, raspberry syrup, honey or even a liqueur.*
2 parts dry (50ml) • *Your dry element is usually your base spirit and gives the drink its main body and strength.*
2 parts wet (50ml) • *Your wet element is your lengthener; it can be soda water, pineapple juice, coconut water or even beer.*

To make a great cocktail it's important to understand the roll these three elements play:

Balance:

A great cocktail has a perfect harmony of flavour. Too much sour element and your drink will be too tart. Too much sweet and you end up with a syrupy mess. Too much dry results in too strong a drink and too much wet element will drown the balance of flavours.

Dilution:

To achieve balance, you must have a level of dilution. If a drink is not diluted enough the heavy flavours can be overwhelming on the first sip, making it a pretty bad experience. But too much dilution and most of the flavours will have disappeared into the watery abyss.

Ice:

This brings us nicely round to the chill factor. Why do bartenders have a crush on ice? Because to get to the holy grail that is balance, you need dilution, and to get dilution... Yep you guessed it, you need ice. Cocktails simply would not work without it. Having ice in the mix during the making of your drink can do everything from changing the temperature to the flavour. A glass filled up with lots of ice is not about selling you short on liquid. In fact, the more ice you have in your glass the colder the drink will stay, aiding the dilution process. Cool, right?

TOOLS OF THE TRADE

So what do you need to make cocktails? The great news is you don't have to spend a small fortune on professional kit There are loads of everyday kitchen items that will do the job.

Saucepans, blenders and juicers, knives, wooden spoons, tea strainers, kitchen scales, chopping boards... You've got the lot hanging around in drawers and cupboards, right?

If you're the extra-inventive type, we're pretty sure you can find some great improvisations. Chopsticks make great stirrers. And if you don't have a set of measuring scales, you could easily use a baby's bottle as a measure. Just make sure you wash it out afterwards!

When it comes to storing your ingredients, you'll need a lot of Tupperware, Kilner jars and swing top bottles, all great for storing citrus juices, syrups, garnishes and the like. It's more cost-effective to make a big batch of the ingredients you'll use more often. You can even make up a load of the same cocktail and store it in the fridge for later.

Talking about inventiveness, here's a top tip for cocktails to go...

Take your homemade mix to the party or the park with our amazing tip. The next time you finish a box of wine, don't throw it away. It's the perfect vessel for cocktails on tap. Open it up, remove the plastic inner, rinse and fill it with your cocktail mix. Seal it back in place with a sandwich bag tie and you're good to go. The little tap you used for your wine will work a treat.

Hawthorne strainer | Bar spoon | Lemons & limes | Shaker | Jigger | Fine strainer | Collins glass

THE LANGUAGE OF COCKTAILS

There are some cocktail skills and methods that are easier if you use professional kit. Each recipe in this book explains the methods and tools you'll need. But first, let's get familiar with some of the terms we use in the trade.

SHAKE:

The cocktail shaker is arguably the most important piece of equipment in any bartender's arsenal. At LCC we use a two-piece tin-on-tin shaker. It's great for speed and never breaks. It's big enough to make multiple drinks in one go, and each one will taste exactly the same.

When you see the instruction 'shake', reach for your cocktail shaker and add all ingredients then the ice.

Hold the shaker firmly with two hands and shake hard and fast every time, ensuring the ice hits both ends of the shaker. The amount of time you shake for depends on the cocktail. A long shake should last 10-12 seconds, when mixing soured classics such as a Daiquiri. A short shake takes 5-6 seconds, which is enough for Espresso Martinis and other drinks that need to be chilled but not diluted (a 12-second shake can add 50ml of dilution to a single cocktail).

Shaking not only mixes a drink, it also chills, dilutes and aerates it. The dilution achieved by shaking is just as important as using the right amount of each ingredient. Too little ice will melt too quickly in the shaker, producing an over-diluted drink and if not shaken enough the drink will not be balanced.

Top Tips:

★ Never shake carbonated liquids like sodas or Champagne. You will end up covered from head to toe in cocktail.

★ Sometimes a drink will call for a 'dry shake'. This comes into play most frequently when using egg whites. Shake without ice for five seconds then add ice and shake for a further five seconds and strain. The result is a nice frothy drink without any unwanted dilution.

★ To open the shaker, bash the point where the two tins meet with the palm of your hand and they should pop right open. Be careful and hold those shakers tight, they can get slippery.

★ Give it a quick taste before you pour into your glass, as this is your last chance to adjust the flavour.

★ If you don't have a shaker to hand, here are some perfectly good substitues: Kilner jar, jam jar, blender (adding two ice cubes per drink can simulate a shake, great when making multiple cocktails at home), protein shaker, or even a bowl and whisk.

THE LANGUAGE OF COCKTAILS

STRAIN:

At LCC we use what's called a Hawthorne strainer to keep the shaken ice/debris from going into the finished drink. When our OCD gets the better of us we also require a basic tea strainer for the perfect finish. Also referred to as a fine strainer, tea strainers remove smaller bits of fruit and fragments of ice which can spoil the appearance of STRAIGHT UP drinks (without ice). It's dead simple, just hold a fine strainer between the shaker/hawthorne and the glass as you pour.

Top Tips:

★ If the tea strainer clogs up, use a small spoon to push through the last of the liquid.
★ For a drink that's been stirred or has a foam, there's no need to bother fine straining.
★ If you don't have a tea strainer to hand, try using a sieve.

BUILD:

Cocktails like the gin and tonic are easy-peasy to make - you simply 'build' them in the glass - in with the ice, gin, then the tonic, give it a little stir and all you need to do is add the garnish and serve.

Top Tips:

★ Pour your spirit and mixer at the same time for consistency.
★ Keep your mixers chilled for the least amount of dilution.

STIR:

The secret of stirred drinks is to get them as cold as possible without diluting too much. Always make sure your equipment is dry (including your ice, it'll dry out in the freezer, wet ice can easily add 25ml of dilution to a single martini) before adding the ingredients.
Combine all ingredients in a 'chilled mixing glass' and stir quickly for 10-15 seconds, aiming for around 30 spins. Strain into a chilled glass. Better to under-stir for a crisp dry finish, than over-stir for a watery mess.

Top Tips:

★ If your budget allows, a thick walled mixing glass is one of my favourite pieces of equipment. However a pint glass or a cafetiere will do just fine.
★ Keep your spirits in the fridge or freezer as the ice will dilute much more slowly.
★ Bar spoons are great if you have one, but latte spoons, chopsticks, and even screwdrivers all get the job done.

MUDDLE:

Muddling is cocktail-speak for squeezing out the juice or flavours from fruits, herbs and spices with, you guessed it... a 'muddler'. If you can't get your hands on one, a rolling pin will do. Put the ingredients in the base of a shaker and push down on the muddler with a twisting action.

Top Tip:

★ You can over-muddle. Use your body weight to push down four/five times on your ingredients to remove the juice without tearing them apart. Let's face it, there is nothing worse than tiny pieces of mint blocking your Mojito straw.

BLEND:

If a cocktail recipe stipulates blend with ice, first place all the ingredients into a blender. Add the recommended amount of ice and give it a whizz until smooth. Blenders are also really useful when making up large quantities of mix before the party starts. It will be big enough to hold 10-15 serves, then leave it in the fridge until you're ready to start shaking.

Top Tip:

★ The perfect consistency for a blended cocktail is like a McDonalds milkshake, it should pour slowly like lava.
★ Adding two ice cubes per drink can simulate a shake, great when making multiple cocktails at home.

LAYER:

Layered drinks are made with different ingredients, often with contrasting colours. Everyone's had a B52, right? To make layers, carefully pour each ingredient into a glass slowly so that it floats on the one before it. It will only work if the liquid below is denser (heavier) than the one on the top. How can you tell? The less alcohol and the more sugar an ingredient has, the heavier it is. So, ingredients should be layered in order of weight with the heaviest at the bottom.

Top Tips:

★ Place a teaspoon so it's touching the previous liquid, and put your thumb firmly over the top of the bottle to dispense slowly. You will spend a lot longer making these than drinking them, but its worth the effort, trust me.
★ To make the whole process easier, I've put a little shortlist (on the next page) of my favoured liqueurs in order of weight. So you're good to go - why not give it a shot?

THE LANGUAGE OF COCKTAILS

To make the whole process easier, I've put a little shortlist of my favoured liqueurs in order of weight. So you're good to go - why not give it a shot? (excuse the pun).

Name	Density
Grenadine	1.18
Crème de Cassis	1.18
Kahlua	1.15
Crème de Banana	1.14
Crème de Cacao	1.14
Coffee Liquor	1.13
Blue Curaçao	1.11
Galliano	1.11
Amaretto	1.10
Tia Maria	1.09
Triple sec	1.09
Drambuie	1.08
Frangelico	1.08
Orange Curaçao	1.08
Campari	1.06
Apricot brandy	1.06
Cherry brandy	1.06
Baileys Irish Cream	1.057
Midori Melon Liquor	1.05
Cherry Liquor	1.04
Cointreau	1.04
Water	1.00
Tuaca	0.98
Southern Comfort	0.97
Vodka (40)	0.92
Absinthe	0.89

BATCHING:

By far one of the most important terms in this book. You can make almost every drink in here up to three days in advance (as long as you refrigerate it).

Simply throw everything in a blender without ice, strain off any pulp or debris, and rest it in the fridge until your time comes to shake it up and serve it. It'll save you a ton of time, and of course pressure. Cooking a dinner party or hosting an event can be stressful enough!

So wash out your empty bottles, and refill them with delicious pre-made cocktails to start your party properly!

GARNISHING:

Garnishing is simply how you finish your drink by adding decoration to it. Different styles of cocktail call for different garnishes, for example tiki rum punches are loud and overstated, where a simple maritini may have no garnish at all. Sometimes it's unclear where the garnish ends and the buffet table begins!

A cocktail is often referred to as the last accessory on a man or woman, and equal to a necklace or watch. So know your audience, you wouldn't catch the Queen sipping from under a paper umbrella.

Top Tips:
- ★ Add a wedge of lemon or lime to your cocktail so that guests can add more citrus if they like.
- ★ Garnishes should represent the nature of the drink, so no rubber ducks in your martinis.
- ★ Use your imagination. Biscuits and sweets can be fun to see and eating them can enhance the experience.

MAKING THE BASICS

Sugar syrups and purées are a key component in cocktails and are not the easiest thing to get hold of. But they are easy enough to make yourself. Here are the syrup hacks we've mastered. They add loads of flavour and will keep in the fridge for a couple of weeks.

When infusing syrups with fruits and herbs, simmer all ingredients in a large pan for 10 minutes on a medium heat (this will vary from spices to herbs, so taste it as you go, spices take much longer). If you want to take your syrups to the next level, cool down the heated mix and blend for 2 minutes before passing through a sieve, this will get the most flavour.

Sugar Syrup Recipe:

500g caster sugar
500ml hot water

In a saucepan add 500ml caster sugar to 500ml of hot water from the kettle, gently simmer until all the sugar has dissolved and the syrup is clear. Let it cool, then pour into an empty bottle and refrigerate (lasts up to 6 weeks).

Top Tips:
- ★ If you're in a rush, simply microwave the mix for 1 minute and give it a stir, it should clear quickly. If not, repeat again.
- ★ Sugar syrup features in a lot of the recipes so make a large batch, you wont regret it.

Simple variants:

- ★ Demerara syrup: 100g of demerara sugar per 100ml hot water.
- ★ Raspberry syrup: Add 50g of fresh raspberries per 100ml of sugar syrup made.
- ★ Lavender syrup: Add 20g of dried lavender per 100ml of sugar syrup made. Pour through a fine strainer after heating to remove the flowers/stalks.
- ★ Earl Grey tea syrup: Add one tea bag per 100ml of sugar syrup made. Simmer for 6 minutes, remove tea bags once cooled.
- ★ Candy shop syrup: Add 25g of Haribo per 100ml of sugar syrup made.
- ★ Polo Mint syrup: Add 1 x 34g pack of Polo Mints per 100ml of sugar syrup made (You may also use Sugar Free Polo Mints to make this syrup).
- ★ Werther's Original syrup: Add 1 x 50g packet of Werther's Original per 100ml of sugar syrup made (You may also use Sugar Free Werther's Original to make this syrup).

- ★ Black Forest purée: Add 600g of frozen black forest or summer fruits to 300ml of sugar syrup made and blend for 1 minute.
- ★ Golden peach purée: Blend one 410g tin of peaches (including the syrup) with 100ml golden syrup for 30 seconds (You may substitute golden syrup with 100ml of honey or sugar syrup).
- ★ Tinned peach purée: Blend one 410g tin of peaches for 30 seconds (including the syrup).

GLASSWARE

Each cocktail should be served in its corresponding glassware/vessel. You may be limited with what you have at home but it's a good idea to have a small selection to play with, and there is a lot of flexibility in this regard.

For example, drinks with citrus or juice (e.g. Cosmopolitan, Clover Club, Apple Martini), which are usually served straight up in a Martini glass can easily be served over cubed ice in a rocks glass. Here is a list of the main glassware used in this book which you can use as a guide:

Martini   Coupe   Collins   Rocks   Shot

Top Tips:
- ★ Where possible always chill your Martini and coupe glasses prior to making the cocktail. You can do this by putting ice cubes in the glass or put the glass in the freezer for 5 minutes so they become frosted, which is a great way to impress your guests.
- ★ Have fun with your glassware/vessels. A few drinks in this book are served in an empty jam jar and you can certainly use these as an alternative to rocks glasses or even highballs if you're stuck.

THE BARTENDER'S DOZEN

One thing that puts people off making cocktails at home and reaching for a beer or a vino instead is the assumption that cocktails are expensive to make. What's more, they demand lots of ingredients of which only a little is needed. That means the rest is wasted or collects dust in the drinks globe.

This section will explain how to get the best bang for your buck and ensure you don't end up throwing half an avocado in the bin.

You will have heard of the baker's dozen, but how about the bartender's dozen? It's not 12, or 13… (they were already taken). I've gone one step further… 14.

The reason for this quirk is simple - most cocktails will use 50ml of the base spirit, and with the standard size of a bottle of hard liquor in the UK being at 70cl, it works out to 14 double measures in every bottle.

Spirits can also be expensive, especially if only making a cocktail for one. So I've knocked up a simple guide to show how to assemble the right ingredients without over or underbuying. So there is no waste if you have too much, and no corner-cutting if you are running short of the key components. Great for a party but you can also make a batch of most of the recipes in this book, store them in some Tupperware or a swing-top bottle and they will keep for a few days in the fridge. No excuses!

So here we go:

1. Work out how big the party is and guestimate how many drinks you think people will have (the better you are at making cocktails the more you'll be making).
2. Say you have 20 guests, all likely to be enjoying two drinks each…
3. Decide on the cocktail or cocktails you want to make and start your shopping list by listing all the ingredients down one side of the page followed by the measurement like I've done below.
4. Then multiply by your guestimated total number of drinks and use the chart below to tell you how many bottles you'll need to buy… Simple!

Let's take the Apple Martini (see page 138) as an example:

- ★ 40ml Vodka
- ★ 40ml Apple juice
- ★ 15ml Honey
- ★ 20ml Apple Sourz
- ★ 20ml Lemon juice
- ★ ¼ Apple (garnish)

THE BARTENDER'S DOZEN

> In our case we have: 20 guests all drinking two cocktails, which gives us 40 cocktails we need to prep for. First we need to know the total amount we'll need of each ingredient simply by multiplying the recipe by the number of serves.

Vodka	40ml	x40	=	1,600ml
Apple Sourz	20ml	x40	=	800ml
Apple juice	40ml	x40	=	1,600ml
Lemon juice	20ml	x40	=	800ml
Honey	15ml	x40	=	600g
Apple	¼	x40	=	10 Apples

The next step is to investigate the size of each bottle or the amount of mint sprigs in a packet for example. Then by dividing our total amounts by the bottle size will tell us exactly how much we need.

1 bottle of Vodka	= 70cl	1,600ml / 700ml	=	2.3 bottles
1 bottle of Apple Sourz	= 70cl	800ml / 700ml	=	1.2 bottles
1 carton of Apple juice	= 1L	1,600ml / 1000ml	=	1.6 cartons
1 lemon (on average) will juice	= 42ml	800ml / 42ml	=	19.1 lemons
1 bottle of honey	= 340g	600g / 340g	=	1.8 bottles
1 bag of apples	= 5 apples	10 / 5	=	2 bags of apples

Problem 1: cl, ml, g, litres... Where in the world you live and what generation you were born into will determine if you're familiar with Imperial or Metric measurement units.

If using recipes from other sources, remember that Americans generally use the US Customary Measurement System or Imperial. Although this makes only marginal differences when it comes to cocktails, it's important to know which you're working with to ensure you're making consistent tasting concoctions. Prior to 1995, the UK used Imperial measurements and as a result some of us still use Imperial units today but whatever you use, this conversion chart will help.

ML	SHOTS	OZ	TSP	TBSP	GRAM
60ml	2 shots	2oz	16	4	60g
42.5ml	1½ shots	1½oz	12	3	42.5g
30ml	1 shot	1oz	8	2	30g
15ml	½ shot	½oz	4	1	15g
10ml	⅓ shot	⅓oz	3	⅔	10g
7.5ml	¼ shot	¼oz	2	½	7.5g
3.75ml	⅛ shot	⅛oz	1	¼	3.75g

`Problem 2:` Watch out when converting millilitres to grams as they are only equal when measuring the volume or weight of water. So for thicker and heavier ingredients like honey it's always best to use scales for accuracy.

Two commonly-used ingredients are lemons and limes. They are extremely versatile and usually used as a garnish to any cocktail that calls for the juice to balance the sweet/citrus. Below shows the yield of each for a variety of common citrus garnishes.

`One lemon`
42ml juice
5 peels
16 slices
8 wheels
8 wedges

`One lime`
30ml juice
4 peels
10 slices
5 wheels
6 wedges

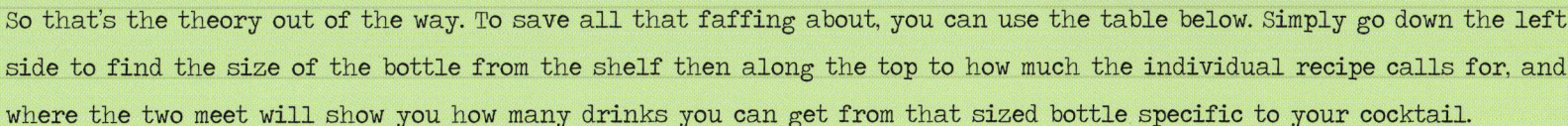

So that's the theory out of the way. To save all that faffing about, you can use the table below. Simply go down the left side to find the size of the bottle from the shelf then along the top to how much the individual recipe calls for, and where the two meet will show you how many drinks you can get from that sized bottle specific to your cocktail.

For example; if the recipe requires 30ml of an ingredient that comes in 500ml bottles, this will quickly show you how many drinks you can get from one bottle. If you're wanting to make more than 16 drinks in this case then you'll need to grab another bottle.

<u>Number of drinks achieved per ingredient</u>

<u>Bottle Size</u>	<u>Unit</u>	<u>5 ml</u>	<u>10 ml</u>	<u>20 ml</u>	<u>25 ml</u>	<u>30 ml</u>	<u>40 ml</u>	<u>50 ml</u>	<u>60 ml</u>
250	ml	50	25	13	10	8	6	5	4
500	ml	100	50	25	20	16	12	10	8
700	ml	140	70	35	28	23	17	14	11
750	ml	150	75	37	30	25	18	15	12
1,000	ml	200	100	50	40	33	25	20	16

THE TEN COMMANDMENTS

Right, before I let you race off to find your favourite cocktail (I know some of you will be jumping straight to 'Party Starters'), let's have a re-cap on the Ten commandments to remember as you set out on the road to becoming a Master of Mixology...

★ 1. Collins Formula: 1 part sour, 1 part sweet, 2 parts dry, 2 parts wet. Stick to this and you can't go wrong.

★ 2. Measuring: If you have them, go for the scales. They are super precise but don't worry if you're a few mls out here or there. It's not the end of the world.

★ 3. The secret to a great drink has little to do with using expensive spirits or the freshest of fruits - although they certainly help. The key is dilution. Having a small amount of dilution is important to take the edge off strong drinks, and for binding the other ingredients together for a consistent drink from start to finish. But don't drown it!

★ 4. Always aim to get the drink as cold as possible. Keep spirits and glassware in the freezer and only take them out at the last second. But don't worry if not, prioritise your martinis first, the rest will taste great straight from the shaker.

★ 5. Time: You want to be mixing up and pouring from shaker, blender etc into the vessel as quick as possible so the drink is at its peak.

★ 6. Balance is vital. What you are looking for in a cocktail is the perfect harmony of flavour. If you have too much of your sour element, your drink will be too tart. If you have too much sweet, you will end up with a syrupy mess. Too much dry, the drink will be too strong and too much wet will mute all the other ingredients.

★ 7. Test every drink you make and as you sip, try for that perfect balance of all four elements - sweet, dry, sour and wet. You can always adjust the cocktail in the shaker before pouring. For example, if it's a little too sour, add a little more sweet to bring it back to the centre.

THE TEN COMMANDMENTS

★ 8. Everyone's heard of the saying 'practise makes perfect'. Well, I'm a firm believer in my own saying: 'proper prior planning prevents piss-poor performance'. Whether you're a professional bartender who's been knocking out classics for years or a newbie looking to make your first Jam Jar Daiquiri, just take a step back and note exactly what you need - from ingredients to glassware and equipment. There is nothing worse than shaking up the cocktail only to realise you left the Hawthorne strainer at your mum's house.

★ 9. Clean as you go: After finishing making a drink, don't just leave the cleaning until later, give it a quick rinse under the tap. You don't know what cocktail you'll be making to follow and it would be a shame to mess up the next masterpiece.

★ 10. Garnish: It can be as simple as a cheeky lime wedge but it's the first thing your mates will notice. The more outrageous the garnish, the more memorable the experience.

***

And I want to see how you're getting on. Tag me on Instagram (@jjgoodmanbartender) with some of your quirky ideas, I would love to see them.

Now, roll up your sleeves, put a pinny on, tie your hair back and get stuck in.

You'll make some mistakes, but learn as you go. Don't be afraid to try different recipes until you find one that clicks.

And most of all, enjoy it. You'll be knocking out cocktails for all your house parties before you know it!

Last but not least, have fun!!!

12-3PM

"Summer punches are typically, but not always, slightly lower in alcohol. Whether you're having a picnic, BBQ or even at a festival, you don't want to bow out too early. This eclectic mix of long and refreshing drinks will no doubt get your day off to the races. If you're feeding the 5,000 at the top of Primrose Hill, you're gonna wanna mix these en masse and march your way into the middle of the party. You're sure to be the star of the show."

DAYTIME SUMMER PUNCHES

FISH HOUSE PUNCH

Mermaids and mermen alike are sure to love this flipping great classic cocktail remastered for your next beach break. So whether you're swimming around or propping up pool-side, be sure to zip up and keep the sand from sailing in.

INGREDIENTS
25ml cognac	£0.98
25ml gold rum	£0.58
25ml lemon juice	£0.18
25ml sugar syrup	£0.03
50ml Lipton peach iced tea	£0.22
Garnish: 3 x Haribo fish sweets	£0.11
Total:	£2.10

EQUIPMENT:
Scales
Spoon
Ziplock bag

METHOD:
Build: pour all ingredients into a ziplock bag with five cubes of ice, seal the bag and shake until cold. Add more ice, garnish & serve. Simples.

SERVED IN:
Ziplock bag

ICE:
Cubed

GARNISH:
3 x Haribo fish sweets

Everyone remembers winning a goldfish at the fair, right?! Only for it to end up in the toilet a few days later. It may seem mad, but in South America, it's not unusual at parties and carnivals to sip your punch from a plain old plastic bag. This drink brings my love for fun vessels and sweet shop garnishes all together, but this time you won't need to flush!

Original Recipe:

FISH HOUSE PUNCH
- 30ml cognac
- 30ml gold rum
- 15ml peach brandy
- 50ml chilled water
- 15ml lemon juice
- 15ml sugar syrup

Traditionally made in large batches, so multiply this recipe depending on how many guests you have. Stir together sugar and water in a large bowl until sugar is dissolved. Add the lemon juice, rum, cognac, and brandy, then add cubed ice (traditionally block ice) and chill down the punch until ready to serve.

History:

Drinks historian David Wondrich once said, the Fish House Punch deserves to be protected by law and taught in schools. He may have a point! Quite possibly the most famous of all punches, it's believed to have been created at the Philadelphia social club called the Schuylkill Fishing Company of Pennsylvania, which was established in 1732. Nobody knows the exact date of the drinks inception; Wondrich says the first written reference to the Fish House Punch appeared in 1794.

WATERMELON CAIPIROSKA

The Caipirinha has a naughty Russian cousin and we love her! This luscious, long, refreshing cocktail is guaranteed to put a smile on your face, so move over "watermelon martini", the Caipiroska is in town, and she's here to stay.

INGREDIENTS	
50ml vodka	£1.05
50g watermelon pulp	£0.02
25ml lemon juice	£0.18
25ml sugar syrup*	£0.03
Garnish	£0.04
Total:	£1.32

★ In a saucepan add 500ml caster sugar to 500ml of hot water from the kettle, gently simmer until all the sugar has dissolved and the syrup is clear. Let it cool, then pour into an empty bottle and refrigerate (lasts up to 6 weeks).

EQUIPMENT:
Scales
Blender
Knife
Chopping board
Large spoon

METHOD:
Blend: Multiply other ingredients in line with how much watermelon you manage to get your hands on. Throw all ingredients into a blender with two cubes of ice per portion and blend. Pour ingredients back into watermelon, turn on the tap and pour to your heart's content.

SERVED IN:
Rocks glass

ICE:
Cubed

GARNISH:
Watermelon triangle

 **SAYS**
If I see a watermelon at a pool party I rush to find a blender to mix my friends this great classic twist. From LA to Ibiza, this one has gone down a treat, and if you have the time to buy a tap online, you'll have everyone talking, drinking and dancing on their sun loungers before you know it!

History:

The 'Caipirinha' (pronounced 'Kie-Pur-Reen-Yah') emerged from the countryside of Sao Paulo during the 19th century, and the name literally translates as "little peasant". It is the national drink of Brazil, and is made with the national spirit of Brazil called Cachaça, which is made from fresh sugar cane juice which is fermented and distilled, much like rum is. However, rum uses molasses which is a by-product of sugar cane refining.

Original Recipe:

CAIPIRINHA (TRADITIONAL RECIPE)

★ 50ml Cachaça
★ 1 whole lime muddled
★ 2 tsp powdered sugar

Cut one lime in to small cubes and muddle in the bottom of a rocks glass with powdered sugar. Add cachaça, fill glass two-thirds with cubed ice and stir well to combine all ingredients. Top with cubed ice and garnish with a lime wheel.

REGGAE
RUM PUNCH

Inspired by the Notting Hill Carnival, this is a real taste of the Caribbean. This drink is normally very sweet and boozy, like the Caribbean itself. We balance ours out with extra citrus to bring it back to London.

INGREDIENTS	
50ml Wray & Nephew rum	£2.40
75ml orange juice	£0.08
75ml pineapple juice	£0.08
25ml lime juice	£0.25
25ml grenadine syrup	£0.15
3 dashes Angostura bitters	£0.15
Garnish	£0.04
Total:	£3.15

EQUIPMENT:
Scales
Mixing spoon
Bar spoon

METHOD:
Build all ingredients into a tin can, add ice and mix with a spoon. Failing that, clean out a watercooler and chuck it all in.

SERVED IN:
Tin can

ICE:
Cubed

GARNISH:
Pineapple leaf
Mint leaf
Cherry
Orange slice

I love the Notting Hill Carnival, who doesn't love dancing in the street!? You can pick up a rum punch on almost every corner. I've drunk rum punches all over the world and I can vouch for the fact that no two recipes are the same. We think ours is the ultimate recipe. And it certainly packs a punch, too.

Original Recipe:

RUM PUNCH

★ 50ml Wray & Nephew rum
★ 15ml grenadine
★ 20ml lime juice
★ 15ml grenadine syrup
★ 45ml orange juice
★ 30ml pineapple juice
★ Juice of 1 small lime
★ 3 dashes Angostura bitters

Shaken and strained over cubed ice into a Collins glass then garnished with a pineapple leaf, cherry and orange slice.

History:

Legendary rum ambassador Ian Burrell created the original Reggae Rum Punch at Arizona Bar in London's famed Camden Town in 1994. Burrell says: "The goal was that the consumer shouldn't realise they are drinking a 63% abv rum, until its too late. By then they'll be singing like Bob Marley (hence the name), yeah mon!". However, it's unlikely that we'll ever know the name of the person who mixed the first bowl of punch (made with brandy), but it was 1707, when Hans Sloane, an English-German physician who travelled to the Caribbean, decided to substitute brandy with the local rum.

JAM JAR DAIQUIRI

Nothing screams summer to me more than strawberries. Either as a kid swatting wasps away from my cheese and jam sandwiches, or these days when Glastonbury festival kicks off in England you'll find me roadside buying punnets off local famers on my long drive up to Worthy Farm. No matter who you're with, this drink is a real crowd-pleaser!

INGREDIENTS

50ml white rum	£1.05
20ml lime juice	£0.20
1 tbsp strawberry jam	£0.10
30ml cranberry juice	£0.03
3 drops vanilla extract	£0.06
Garnish	£0.13
Total:	**£1.57**

EQUIPMENT:
Scales
Mixing spoon

METHOD:
Add all ingredients into the jam jar with two cubes of ice, pop the lid on and shake this drink REALLY hard! Add more ice once shaken and garnish. Or just bang it all in the blender.

SERVED IN:
Jam jar

ICE:
Cubed

GARNISH:
Strawberry Haribo sweets
Lime wedge
Mint sprig

Our jammy version was invented in our early days, from necessity. We couldn't afford to waste fresh fruit, so jam was cheaper, more consistent, and didn't go off! The pectins used in jams happen to give the drink a great mouth feel, making this a true LCC legend. Don't stop with strawberry, as apricot or raspberry jams will slot into this recipe with ease!

Original Recipe:

DAIQUIRI (COX'S RECIPE)

★ 60ml white rum
★ juice of 1 small lime
★ 2 tsp superfine sugar

Squeeze the juice of 1 lime into a highball, add the sugar and stir to dissolve, fill glass with cracked ice, add 60ml of white rum and stir. No garnish.

History:

Quite possibly the most globally recognised cocktail along with the Mojito, and a bartender's go-to drink. Like many other cocktails the Daiquiri has an uncertain past. The story, which seems the most accurate, is of American engineer Jennings Cox who came up with this drink whilst leading a mining team into the small town of Daiquiri, Cuba in 1898. The drink was originally served in a tall glass packed with cracked ice. A teaspoon of sugar was poured over the ice and the juice of one or two limes was squeezed over the sugar, and a large measure of rum added.

PIÑA COLADA

This is a holiday in a glass! A tropical blend of rich coconut cream, white rum and tangy pineapple that we all know and love. Sip it back, close your eyes and smell the suncream, as a nice big hit of sugary goodness will certainly get you in the mood to party!

INGREDIENTS	
50ml Malibu	£1.05
50ml gold rum	£1.15
90ml pineapple juice	£0.09
50ml creamed coconut	£0.25
25ml sugar syrup*	£0.03
Garnish	£0.06
Total:	£2.63

EQUIPMENT:
Scales
Blender

METHOD:
Bang it all in the blender with five cubes of ice per serve.

SERVED IN:
Hurricane glass

ICE:
None

GARNISH:
Pineapple triangle
Cherry
Pineapple leaf

★ In a saucepan add 500ml caster sugar to 500ml of hot water from the kettle, gently simmer until all the sugar has dissolved and the syrup is clear. Let it cool, then pour into an empty bottle and refrigerate (lasts up to 6 weeks).

You can't help but feeling like "Del Boy" with a fully garnished Piña Colada in your hand, but that's never put me off. I've been lucky enough to go to the home of this drink, Puerto Rico, where it practically pours from the sky. This is every bartender's guilty pleasure and it should be yours too!

Original Recipe:

PIÑA COLADA

★ 50ml gold rum
★ 50ml fresh pineapple juice
★ 25ml Coco Lopez cream of coconut
★ 25ml double cream

Blend with a cup of crushed ice for 20 seconds. Pour into a hurricane glass. Garnish with a pineapple triangle and a red maraschino cherry.

History:

Piña Colada literally means 'strained pineapple', which references the freshly strained pineapple juice used in the drink's recipe. Bartender Ramon 'Monchito' Perez claims to have created this much-loved classic at the Caribe Hilton Hotel's Beachcomber Bar in San Juan, Puerto Rico back in 1952, using the newly available Coco Lopez cream of coconut.

BRAMLEY APPLE SMASH

If you love apple sauce with your Sunday roast, then you will adore this summertime cocktail that combines the freshness of mint, the floral notes of gin and elderflower with the sensationally nostalgic taste of Bramley apple sauce.

INGREDIENTS

50ml gin	£1.05
25ml lemon juice	£0.18
25ml elderflower cordial	£0.18
25ml Bramley apple sauce	£0.20
50ml apple juice	£0.05
6 mint leaves	£0.06
Garnish	£0.05
Total:	**£1.77**

EQUIPMENT:
Scales
Spoon

METHOD:
Shake and strain: add all ingredients into the jam jar with two cubes of ice, pop the lid on and shake. Add more ice and garnish.

SERVED IN:
Jam jar

ICE:
Cubed

GARNISH:
2 custard cream biscuits

The only thing missing from this recipe is the pork bap! Bramley apple sauce is a favourite of mine, it ought to be dripping out of a white bread roll while you crunch down on crackling, stuffing and juicy pork belly, but I promise you we've done it justice here. Big shout out to my boy Andy Mil for this truly English concoction.

Original Recipe:

THE REAL MINT JULEP (Jerry Thomas)

★ 60ml brandy or peach brandy
★ 1 tbsp of white pulverized sugar
★ 2 tbsp water
★ 3-4 sprigs of mint
★ Dash Jamaican rum

Add mint sugar and water to a rocks glass. Press the mint into the sugar and water until the flavour of the mint is extracted. Add brandy and fill with fine shaved ice. Churn with a spoon, add dash of rum and garnish with a mint sprig.

History:

The Bramley Apple Smash was created in 2010 by London Cocktail Club bartending legend Andy Mil. One of the earliest examples of a smash appears in the form of 'The Real Mint Julep' recipe in the 1862 book How to Mix Drinks, by Jerry Thomas, using both peach and common brandy. The mint julep we know today (bourbon, mint and sugar) has been the official drink of the Kentucky Derby since 1938. If you want a handcrafted mint julep served in a pewter cup at this famous horse race, be prepared to part with $1,000! Cha-ching!

SEX ON THE BEACH

As my love for guilty pleasures continues, I can't miss out this classic cocktail that always makes me giggle. It's fruity, light, sweet and dry, with a legendary blend of peach and cranberry. Don't be too cool for school, mix a fresh batch up today!

INGREDIENTS

25ml vodka	£0.53
25ml peach schnapps	£0.45
50ml golden peach purée*	£0.07
50ml cranberry juice	£0.05
2 dashes absinthe	£0.12
10ml lemon juice	£0.07
2 drops vanilla extract	£0.04
Garnish	£0.10
Total:	**£1.43**

★ Golden peach purée: Blend one 410g tin of peaches (including the syrup) with 100ml golden syrup for 30 seconds (You may substitute golden syrup with 100ml of honey or sugar syrup).

EQUIPMENT:
Scales
Mixing spoon

METHOD:
Add all the ingredients to your Collins glass, fill with cubed ice and stir well.

SERVED IN:
Collins glass

ICE:
Cubed

GARNISH:
Lemon wheel
Cherry
Orange wedge

JJ SAYS: LCC superstar Andy Mil and I helped drive the "Twisted Disco" movement way back in 2010. With our tongues in our cheeks, we took our favourite disco classics and added a contemporary twist to revitalise them. The fact is that the classic pairing of peach and cranberry works, but it needed "pimping", so along came white peach purée, our love of absinthe, and after a tinkering of measurements that Andy's famous for, we put the sex, back in the Sex On The Beach!

Original Recipe:

SEX ON THE BEACH

- ★ 50ml vodka
- ★ 20ml peach schnapps
- ★ 40ml orange juice
- ★ 40ml cranberry juice

Add all ingredients to a shaker, fill with cubed ice, shake and strain into a tall glass filled with cubed ice. Garnish with a slice of orange.

History:

Also a popular song in 1997 (by T-Spoon), this cocktail was born in the 1980s at Florida's Confetti Bar at a time when cocktail names often had some kind of sexual terminology attached. The drink was named 'Sex on the Beach' because "sex" and "the beach" were the two main reasons why spring breakers (the bar's main clientele in Florida) visited the state. God bless the eighties!

SANGRIA

Anyone who's had tapas in Spain, especially in Barcelona where the restaurants on Las Ramblas spill into the streets, and the energy and excitement are as infectious as the sangria, will know that this drink is as important a taste of Spain as the paella on your plate!

INGREDIENTS (SERVES 10)

1 x bottle young red Rioja wine	£10.00
250ml Spanish brandy	£5.00
200ml orange juice	£0.20
330ml lemonade	£0.50
3 cracked cinnamon sticks	£0.08
5 star anise	£0.40
5 cherries	£0.05
150ml demerara sugar syrup*	£0.15
12 mint leaves	£0.08
½ lemon, sliced	£0.15
½ orange/blood orange, sliced	£0.15
½ apple, sliced	£0.15
Total:	**£16.91**
	(£1.69 per serve)

★ In a saucepan add 100ml demerara sugar to 100ml of hot water from the kettle, gently simmer until all the sugar has dissolved. Let it cool, then pour into an empty bottle and refrigerate (lasts up to 6 weeks).

Original Recipe:

SANGRIA

- ★ 60ml dry red wine
- ★ 20ml cognac
- ★ 20ml orange juice
- ★ 1 tsp caster sugar
- ★ 2 lemon slices
- ★ 2 orange slices
- ★ 2 apple slices

Mix with cubed ice into a punch bowl or jug before serving into wine glasses. Garnish with a slice of orange.

EQUIPMENT:
Measuring jug
Scales
Wooden spoon

METHOD:
Build by placing all ingredients in punch bowl with 400g of ice (20 cubes) and stir gently until thoroughly mixed.

SERVED IN:
Punch bowl
Punch glasses

ICE:
Cubed

GARNISH:
Fruit & spices from the mix

JT SAYS

My trips to Spain are dominated by food, friends and drinks. And although everyone loves a sangria, few have transported a great recipe back home. For me, the secret is brandy; I've gone easy on it in this recipe, but feel free to turn up the heat. If you're still having trouble add a touch more sugar, it makes cheaper wines easier to drink while bringing out all the other flavours.

History:

The name of this traditional Spanish red wine punch means blood, as the drink is red in colour. The history of Sangria goes back, and we mean way, way back! Early Greeks and Romans mixed their wine with sugar, spices, and whatever else was on hand. It was called "hippocras," and it was sometimes heated like mulled wine, meaning it was probably the common ancestor of both sangria and mulled wine. This beverage was drunk everywhere because water in the Middle Ages was unfit for human consumption. A touch of alcohol made the liquid drinkable, and mixing the watered-down wine with seasonal fruits, berries and spices gave it flavour.

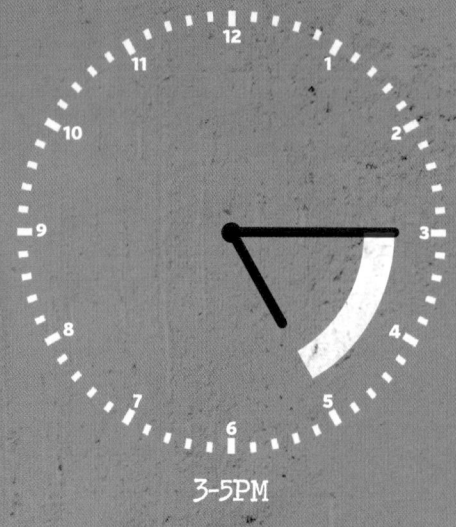

3-5PM

"Not just reserved for your package holidays in the south of Spain, these spritzers and shandies are perfect for those wanting a Champagne lifestyle on a lemonade budget. Often frowned upon by many mixology maestros, these bubbly, boozy beverages are not only easy to make but will often convert the most hesitant cocktail critic. From the hills of Hogwarts to the canals of Venice, here you'll find something for everyone."

SPRITZERS & SHANDIES

BELLINI

'Sophistication in a glass! Prosecco and peach purée or nectar is all it takes to create this long refreshing classic cocktail that is sure to make you say "aaaaaaargh"!

INGREDIENTS	
100ml prosecco	£0.90
25ml golden peach purée*	£0.06
Garnish	£0.03
Total:	£0.99

★ Golden peach purée: Blend one 410g tin of peaches (including the syrup) with 100ml golden syrup for 30 seconds (You may substitute golden syrup with 100ml of honey or sugar syrup).

EQUIPMENT:
Scales
Spoon
Mixing glass
Blender

METHOD:
Build. Pour 25ml of tinned peach purée into the bottom of a flute and top with prosecco and give a very gentle stir.

SERVED IN:
Flute glass

ICE:
None

GARNISH:
Tinned peach slice
Sprig of thyme

 Venice, Italy is truly a magical place. Getting off the plane and hopping straight on to one of the many beautiful polished wood water taxis, heading down the Grand Canal, under the stunning bridges, passing by the incredible architecture, listening to the opera-singing gondoliers is a memory I'll never forget. The highlight of course was Harry's Bar overlooking the water in San Marco. If it's not on your bucket list please add it on, as the journey alone is worth the trip.

History:

The Bellini was invented in the mid 1900s by Giuseppe Cipriani, founder of Harry's Bar in Venice, Italy, a favourite haunt of Ernest Hemingway and Orson Welles. The drinks name refers to its unique colour, which reminded Giuseppe of a toga worn by a saint in a painting by 15th-century Venetian artist Giovanni Bellini. The drink started as a seasonal speciality, however it also became popular at the bar's New York counterpart. After an entrepreneurial Frenchman set up a business to ship fresh white 'Verona' peach purée to both locations, it became a year-round favourite.

Original Recipe:

BELLINI

★ 30ml peach purée
★ 80ml prosecco

Add peach purée to a flute, pour chilled prosecco on top, and gently stir. No garnish.

ELDERFLOWER GARDEN PARTY

This super sipper is a guaranteed crowd pleaser. Once you've made one of these you'll never need your corkscrew again. Move over Sauvignon and Chardonnay, the Elderfower Garden Party is here to stay!

INGREDIENTS

30ml vodka	£0.63
10ml elderflower cordial	£0.07
5ml runny honey	£0.04
50ml apple juice	£0.05
50ml cava	£0.45
10ml lemon juice	£0.07
Garnish	£0.03
Total:	£1.34

EQUIPMENT:
Scales
Spoon
Mixing glass

METHOD:
Build. Add ingredients (except cava) to wine glass, add cubed ice, stir, and then top with cava. You may multiply the recipe and dispense through a clean watering can to impress your friends.

SERVED IN:
Wine glass
Or watering can

ICE:
Cubed

GARNISH:
Cucumber peel
Mint sprig

 **SAYS** In the battle of wine and beer versus cocktails, we developed a range of mixed drinks with some of our favourite tasting notes from classic wine varieties like Sauvignon Blanc, Chardonnay and Riesling. This one stood out as it's too easy to drink, super simple to make and CHEAPER than any wine that could possibly match its bursting flavour. So if you're up for a drink that's long, sour with a subtle sweetness, then this one is for you!

Original Recipe:

SPRITZER
★ 125ml white wine
★ 50ml soda water

Build and serve in a wine glass with ice cubes (optional).

History:

The Spritzer dates all the way back to 1842 and the country of Hungary. Legend has it, Hungarian author András Fáy invited some friends to visit his new wine cellar, one of them brought along a bottle of soda water. Since the newly invented soda water was all the rage in those days, András decided to mix it with the white wine he was pouring, and upon drinking his new creation, decided to call the drink a Spritzer.

BLACKCURRANT SOUFFLÉ

You'll love the theatre of watching this "silver fizz" foam up in front of your guests, and it's a great alternative for the classic French dessert that will keep you wanting more!

INGREDIENTS

40ml vodka	£0.84
50ml Champagne	£1.30
20ml lemon juice	£0.14
30ml Black Forest purée*	£0.12
20ml sugar syrup	£0.02
30g egg white	£0.15
Garnish	£0.01
Total:	**£2.58**

★ Black Forest purée: Add 600g of frozen Black Forest or summer fruits and 300ml of sugar syrup and blend.

EQUIPMENT:
Scales
Cocktail shaker
Hawthorne strainer
Fine strainer

METHOD:
Shake first five ingredients and fine strain into a chilled coupe then top with Champagne.

SERVED IN:
Coupe glass

ICE:
None

GARNISH:
Mint Leaf

 **JL SAYS**

This is the cocktail I won BBC2's The Restaurant with in 2009. In the dying moments of the final episode it really saved us from certain elimination as I managed to totally screw up the actual soufflé that I was tasked to make. Fortunately the ingredients are almost exactly the same (just add booze), shake rather than bake, then "supercharge" any classic sour cocktail with Champagne and you'll have a "silver fizz" that will rise like a soufflé every time!

Original Recipe:

SILVER GIN FIZZ

★ 60ml gin
★ 25ml lemon juice
★ 20ml sugar syrup
★ 15ml egg white
★ 50ml soda water

Shake the first four ingredients, strain into a tall glass (no ice), top with soda. Garnish with a lemon wheel.

History:

The first printed recipe for a Gin Fizz appeared in legendary cocktail book Jerry Thomas's Bartender's Guide in 1876. Similarly, the Boston Globe offered instructions on making a Gin Fizz in 1882, and by that point several variations of this drink were flying over bars across the country. The Silver Gin Fizz has the addition of egg white to give it a silky smooth texture, however it's unknown who created it or when. It was a very popular cocktail in New Orleans, where variations such as the Ramos Gin Fizz were invented.

PIMM'S ROYAL

'Ace!' Nothing screams Royal Britannia more than Wimbledon's grass court tennis tournament. If you're ready to upgrade from the classic Pimm's Cup, then this bubblie belter is just for you!

INGREDIENTS

35ml Pimm's	£0.70
75ml Lanson Champagne	£3.23
1 orange slice	£0.02
1 diced strawberry	£0.17
1 small cucumber slice	£0.02
1 small lemon slice	£0.02
3 mint leaves	£0.02
5ml lemon juice	£0.04
15ml Robinsons blackcurrant cordial	£0.02
Garnish	£0.10
Total:	**£4.34**

EQUIPMENT:
Scales
Spoon
Mixing glass
Glass jug

METHOD:
Build. Add all the ingredients  (except the Champagne) to your mixing glass filled with cubed ice, stir and then strain into a flute, carefully topping up with Champagne. You can multiply this recipe and serve in a glass jug for sharing with friends.

SERVED IN:
Flute glass
Glass jug

ICE:
Cubed

GARNISH:
Half a strawberry
Mint sprig
Slice of cucumber

Original Recipe:

PIMM'S CUP
★ 50ml Pimm's No. 1 Cup
★ 60ml lemonade
★ 60ml ginger ale
★ 6 mint leaves
★ 1 slice of orange
★ 1 fresh strawberry
★ 1 slice cucumber

Add all ingredients except the lemonade and ginger ale to a tall glass. Fill with cubed ice, add lemonade and ginger ale, gently stir (lifting fruit from the bottom). Garnish with slices of orange, lemon and cucumber, sliced strawberry and borage.

 A day out at Wimbledon is the most stereotypical, British event of the year, followed closely by Henley Regatta, polo in the park and of course Cheltenham races. That said, I love all the above. I'll shamelessly be seen in white chinos, blue blazer and one too many buttons undone on my shirt, while a massive pair of sunglasses disguises my already glazed-over eyes from the midday sun and onlooking "punters"!

History:
The original Pimm's Cup was created in 1840 by James Pimm. The tawny-coloured gin-based liquor Pimm's No. 1 Cup is the foundation of the infamous cocktail. James Pimm, the landlord of Pimm's Oyster House on Lombard Street in London's financial district, invented and marketed it as a health tonic. The mixture became so popular over the next decade that Pimm then began selling his secret concoction commercially and then globally.

BOILERMAKERS

Whether you sip, shoot or depth charge, you can all ways rely on a boilermaker to get you up and at 'em. Here's some of my favourite pairings to get you going, while appreciating the finer things in life.

INGREDIENTS	
330ml bottle/can of ale	£1.30
25ml Scotch whisky	£0.54
Total	£1.84
330ml bottle/can of stout	£1.30
25ml Irish whiskey	£0.63
Total	£1.93
330ml bottle of lager	£0.95
25ml Bourbon whiskey	£0.65
Total	£1.60
330ml bottle of cider	£1.10
25ml Calvados	£1.10
Total	£2.20

EQUIPMENT:
Scales

METHOD:
Build. Pour your choice of beer slowly into a chilled Collins glass, and serve the whisk(e)y on the side. If you feel like depth-charging, drop your choice of whisk(e)y into your beer.

SERVED IN:
Collins glass
Shot glass

ICE:
None

GARNISH:
None

I start and finish any big night out with a boilermaker! I'll sip the beer, shoot my shot and wait for my "sour" to arrive (normally a daiquiri). My last order of the night, I like to spoil myself with a top shelf spirit, while nursing an ale, and wait for my taxi to take me back to bed.

Original Recipe:

BOILERMAKER (ENGLISH)
★ ½ pint draught lager
★ ½ pint bottled brown ale

Mix the two together in a pint glass.

BOILERMAKER (AMERICAN)
★ Pint of beer
★ Shot of bourbon

Drop the shot into the beer and drink.

History:

The Oxford English Dictionary explains the term "boilermaker" was first used to refer to the men employed to make and repair boilers or other heavy metal items in the 1800s. Nobody really knows who invented the boilermaker cocktail, but it's seems likely the drink takes its name from these craftsmen, as they headed to the bar at the end of their shift. A shot of whisky with a beer quenched their thirst and eased the aches that came from a day of back-breaking labour. In England, the term boilermaker traditionally refers to a half pint of draught mild lager mixed with a half pint of bottled brown ale.

GUINNESS PUNCH

"Do you want to put a flake in that pint?!", well yes, this time I do! Creamy, rich and spicy, this twisted classic isn't just for Paddy's Day "to be sure".

INGREDIENTS

25ml Irish whiskey	£0.63
75ml Guinness	£0.23
30g condensed milk	£0.12
Pinch of cinnamon	£0.02
Pinch of nutmeg	£0.02
3 drops vanilla extract	£0.06
Garnish	£0.23
Total:	**£1.31**

EQUIPMENT:
Scales
Cocktail shaker
Hawthorne strainer

METHOD:
Shake and strain.

SERVED IN:
Half-pint Guinness glass

ICE:
Cubed

GARNISH:
Whipped cream
Chocolate flake
Pinch of nutmeg

JJ SAYS: I love a Jamaican-style Guinness punch, but it always struck me as strange that there isn't an Irish version?! Fear not, as my favourite Irishman, Aaron Wall and I sat down to create the ultimate! I love a creamy drink, and those vanilla flavours in condensed milk are PERFECT for almost any creamy classic. The Irish whiskey brings this cocktail back home to its native Dublin where it belongs.

Original Recipe:

IRISH MILK PUNCH

★ 50ml Irish whiskey
★ 150ml milk
★ 2 tsp honey
★ 1/8 tsp ground ginger
★ 1/8 tsp ground cinnamon

Add all ingredients to a saucepan and stir on a medium heat (do not let it boil). Pour into a mug and top with grated nutmeg.

History:

Scailtín, which is Gaelic for Irish Milk Punch, is a beverage dating back to the 1700s. By using alcohol as a preservative, the beverage was often sold bottled. It became such a popular drink that even Queen Victoria was an advocate, and in 1838 she awarded her favourite bottled version, which was made by Nathaniel Whisson & Co, the title of 'Purveyors of Milk Punch to Her Majesty'. Now that is some honour! Slàinte!

BUTTER BEER

Trust me when I tell you that not even Hogwarts could teach a better recipe, with or without a wand. I've boozed up this beverage with bourbon, caramel, apples and vanilla flavours topped off with a classic London ale.

INGREDIENTS

50ml bourbon	£1.30
45ml dark ale	£0.18
15ml Werther's Original syrup*	£0.12
25ml apple juice	£0.03
2 drops vanilla extract	£0.04
30g egg white	£0.15
Total:	**£1.82**

★ Werther's Original syrup: Add 1 x 50g packet of Werther's Original per 100ml of sugar syrup made (You may also use Sugar Free Werther's Original to make this syrup).

EQUIPMENT:
Scales
Cocktail shaker
Hawthorne strainer

METHOD:
Add all ingredients to shaker filled with cubed ice, shake and strain into half pint glass.

SERVED IN:
Half pint glass

ICE:
Cubed

GARNISH:
None

 **JL SAYS**

I love my movies, and JK Rowling left us all with this gift of a series. I'm bringing a taste of "The Leaky Cauldron" into your muggle lives with this drink straight out of the wizarding world. This was a drink we mixed time and time again until we finally nailed the perfect blend; it's easily the best recipe out there!

Original Recipe:

HOT BUTTERED RUM

★ 50ml dark rum
★ 2 tsp runny honey
★ 1 knob of butter
★ 1 tsp ground nutmeg
★ Boiling water to top up

In a toddy glass add the first four ingredients, then top up with boiling water and stir until the butter has dissolved and everything is combined. Garnish with a cinnamon stick and a lemon wheel studded with cloves.

History:

Butter beer was coined by JK Rowling in the Harry Potter novels, however, the first drink known to make use of butter dates back to colonial times in the United States. It was in the 1650s when Jamaica began importing molasses to Colonial America and New Englanders started distilling it, utilising rum in cold weather drinks such as hot toddies. It wasn't long before they were adding butter and spices to enrich these drinks, thus creating the hot buttered rum. Our friends across the pond love this drink so much they celebrate every year on 17th January with National Hot Buttered Rum Day!

DOCTOR PEPPER

The simple "shandy" may not make your eyes light up in wonder, and that's because you're not mixing them right! Beer, like wine, makes for an incredible mixer when blending cocktails, and this classic shooter is just as fun to sip as it is to gulp!

INGREDIENTS
- 25ml amaretto £0.60
- 75ml lager £0.30
- 75ml Coca-Cola £0.08

Total: £0.98

EQUIPMENT:
Scales

METHOD:
Build: add the lager and Coca-Cola to a half pint glass and when you're ready, drop a shot glass of amaretto in the top and off you go.

SERVED IN:
Half pint glass
Shot glass

ICE:
None

GARNISH:
None

Original Recipe:

LAGER SHANDY
- ★ 300ml lager
- ★ 250ml lemonade

SNAKEBITE
- ★ 250ml lager
- ★ 250ml cider
- ★ 50ml blackcurrant cordial

BLACK VELVET
- ★ 300ml Guinness
- ★ 250ml Champagne

TURBO SHANDY
- ★ 300ml lager
- ★ Topped up with Smirnoff Ice

SHANDY GAFF
- ★ 350ml lager
- ★ Topped up with ginger ale

MONACO
- ★ 300ml lager
- ★ 200ml lemonade
- ★ 50ml grenadine

This was the shooter of choice working at Be At One in Battersea for my then GM Deano Scupham. When we were five deep at the bar pouring our hearts out for the eagerly waiting customers, I'd always smile when this refreshing little number would appear on my bar top. It was his way of saying well done, keep going, and it transports me back every time I have one.

History:

In France they call it Panache, in Spain they call it Clara, and in the UK we call it shandy. The word "shandy" comes from an old British drink known as a "shandygaff," this drink first appeared in the 1850s and is a combination of beer mixed with ginger ale. The name comes from the London slang for a pint of beer, 'shant of gatter' (shant meaning pub, gatter meaning water). It therefore predates the radler (beer and lemonade), which Bavarian tavern owner Franz Kugler invented out of necessity in 1922 when his daily supply of beer was running low.

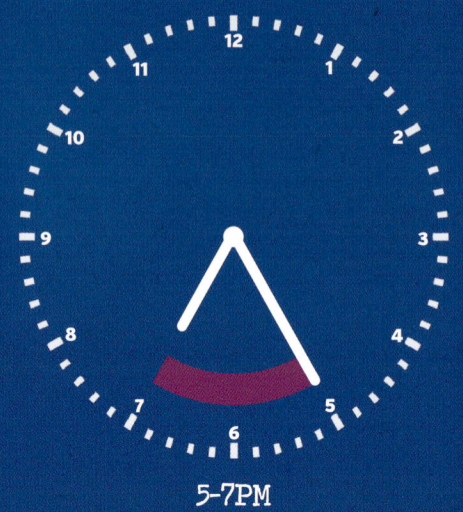

5-7PM

"We boozy Brits love to whet our appetites, but it's our European cousins who have perfected the art of preparing the palate. However, I've stolen my favourite palate cleansers and brought them back to Blighty with some original twists of my own. When the sun starts to set over the yardarm, mix up one of these to celebrate the end of the day and the start of the night."

APERITIFS

GIBSON MARTINI

James Bond's favourite martini was the shaken, not stirred "Vesper", mine is the Gibson. Ice cold, bone dry martinis are a rite of passage for any booze buff, but adding the refreshing bite of a pickled onion between mouthfuls is easily the tastiest tipple on the market.

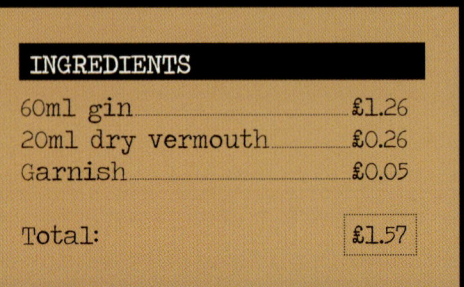

INGREDIENTS	
60ml gin	£1.26
20ml dry vermouth	£0.26
Garnish	£0.05
Total:	£1.57

EQUIPMENT:
Scales
Spoon
Mixing glass
Hawthorne strainer

METHOD:
Stir. Add all ingredients to mixing glass filled with ice, stir and then strain into chilled martini glass.

SERVED IN:
Martini glass

ICE:
None

GARNISH:
Silverskin onion

JL SAYS: This drink is a classic example of how the simplest drinks are hardest to perfect, and the trick to the perfect martini is to ensure the drink is as cold as possible with minimal dilution. So, freeze the gin beforehand. And 'wash' your ice cubes with vermouth to ensure only the toughest ice is in your mixing glass. The noise of ice stirred in a mixing glass, clinking from side to side, is one that will always make my ears prick up with excitement!

Original Recipe:

MARTINEZ
★ 50ml gin
★ 10ml dry vermouth
★ 15ml sweet vermouth
★ 5ml maraschino liqueur
★ 1 dash Angostura bitters

Stir ingredients before serving in a vintage Martini glass with an orange twist.

History:

The Gibson's history is as mysterious as the Bermuda Triangle. The oldest published recipe for the Gibson dates back to 1908. Our favourite story involves a well-known graphic artist named Charles Dana Gibson who was famous for his "Gibson Girl" illustrations, which were as iconic as the supermodels of today. Unsurprisingly Gibson was a member of the New York Players Club where he is thought to have challenged bartender Charley Conolly to come up with a new cocktail for him. It's believed the drink was named after the big-bosomed Gibson Girls, hence the two onions on the garnish. Wink, wink.

ZAZA

Her majesty the Queen's favourite tipple - and one of many of her mother's before her - the royals have one of these aperitifs daily before lunch! Mostly dry, slightly sweet and filthy rich, the drink's description could almost match that of Lizzie herself. God save the Queen!

INGREDIENTS
50ml gin	£1.05
25ml Dubonnet red	£0.30
Garnish	£0.06
Total:	£1.41

EQUIPMENT:
Scales
Spoon
Mixing glass
Hawthorne strainer

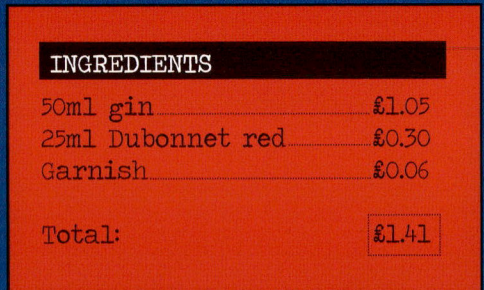

METHOD:
Stir. Add all ingredients to mixing glass filled with cubed ice, stir and strain into chilled sherry glass.

SERVED IN:
Small sherry glass

ICE:
None

GARNISH:
Orange twist

I've been lucky enough to mix cocktails at Buckingham Palace where I presented in the gardens on the drinking habits of the royal family. They took it lightly and saw the funny side. The few days for the Royal Warrant holders' fair was a massive success! Getting to be stage side watching the national orchestra play in the evening is a memory I'll never forget, though the secrets of the royals ought to stay with me and off the pages of this book!

Original Recipe:
ZAZA
- ★ 30ml gin
- ★ 60ml Dubonnet red
- ★ Dash of Angostura bitters (optional)

Shake and serve into a coupe glass. Garnish with an orange twist.

History:

Created for Harry Craddock's 1930 Savoy Cocktail Book, this drink was named after a French play which was a hit at the turn of the century, followed by opera and film versions. However, the most intriguing aspect of the Zaza's history is its presence within the royal family. Major Colin Burgess, who was the personal attendant to the Queen, says she would start drinking each day at noon with a cocktail made up of one part gin and two parts Dubonnet, finished with a slice of lemon or orange depending on her mood.

LAVENDER PALOMA

Mexico's second favourite tipple has been remastered to make it its first! Let the lovely long-lasting linger of lavender balance perfectly with the tequila, honey and grapefruit for a flavour that you'll never want to end.

INGREDIENTS

35ml tequila	£0.91
10ml lime juice	£0.10
10ml homemade lavender syrup*	£0.17
35ml grapefruit juice	£0.04
10ml runny honey	£0.08
100ml prosecco	£0.90
Garnish	£0.13
Total:	£2.33

★ Lavender syrup: In a saucepan add 20g of dried lavender for every 100ml of sugar syrup mix. Simmer on a medium heat for 6 minutes. Let the mixture cool, pour through a sieve or fine strainer into an empty bottle or kilner jar to remove the flowers/stalks and refrigerate (lasts up to 6 weeks).

EQUIPMENT:
Scales
Cocktail shaker
Hawthorne strainer

METHOD:
Shake top five ingredients, strain over cubed ice and top with prosecco.

SERVED IN:
Wine glass

ICE:
Cubed

GARNISH:
Grapefruit twist
Lavender sprig

JL SAYS: This drink always reminds me of the time spent with Raymond Blanc working the kitchens at Le Manoir Aux Quat'Saisons, where lavender lines every walkway all year round and its smell is the first thing that hits you when you step foot on to that extraordinary fairytale mansion. The drink itself originated from Craft Cocktail Co back in 2014 by Matt Armitage (one of my favourite palates in the industry). Matt often created ingenious twists on classic cocktails as only a true master can, and I fell in love at first sip with this beauty.

Original Recipe:

PALOMA

★ 50ml tequila
★ 20ml pink grapefruit juice
★ 20ml lime juice
★ 15ml agave nectar
★ 100ml grapefruit soda

Build with cubed ice and serve into a Collins glass with a salt rim. Garnish with a pink grapefruit wedge.

History:

The Paloma (meaning dove in Spanish) is the most popular tequila-based cocktail in Mexico and a favourite with bartenders the world over. It's believed to have been created by the legendary Don Javier Delgado Corona, who was the owner and bartender of La Capilla (The Chapel), in the small town of Tequila in Mexico around the 1960s. It was popularised by the soda brand "Squirt" who were known as the original mixer, and they began marketing it globally soon after.

NEGRONI

Bitter but certainly not twisted, the Negroni is a classic cocktail that every great bartender knows and loves. As Italian as pizza, pasta and even Andrea Pirlo, sit back and sip away with the sunset to your heart's content.

INGREDIENTS	
40ml gin	£0.84
20ml Campari	£0.44
20ml sweet vermouth	£0.12
Splash of soda (optional)	£0.02
Garnish	£0.06
Total:	£1.48

EQUIPMENT:
Scales
Spoon

METHOD:
Stir. Add all ingredients to rocks glass and stir. Add a splash of soda to lengthen if desired.

SERVED IN:
Rocks glass

ICE:
Cubed

GARNISH:
Orange twist

I've always preferred a 2:1:1 ratio of double gin in my Negronis and I'm sure you will too (classically it's even measures of each). It's a drink that's blown up to worldwide popularity, and you'll either love or hate its bittersweet character. I'll often ask for a small bottle of soda on the side to lengthen it so I make sure it lasts a little longer, and doesn't knock me out before I've even sat down to eat.

Original Recipe:

AMERICANO
- 25ml sweet vermouth
- 25ml Campari
- 100ml soda

Stir in a Collins glass with some cubed ice. Garnish with an orange slice.

History:

Invented at Caffe Casoni in Florence, Italy in 1919. Legend has it Count Camillo Negroni asked bartender Forsco Scarselli, to strengthen his favourite cocktail, the Americano, by replacing the soda water with gin. The drink was an instant hit! Before long, everyone was coming into the bar for a 'Negroni'. The Negroni family quickly took advantage of the cocktail's success, founding the Negroni Distillery later that same year, in Treviso, Italy, where they produced a ready-made version of the drink, sold as Antico Negroni.

WATERLOO SUNSET

This is the gateway drink to becoming a bitter-loving booze-hound. It's softer on the palate than its big brothers the Negroni and Aperol Spritz, with gentle sweetness and mouth-quenching juices taking it to the next level!

INGREDIENTS

25ml gin	£0.53
15ml Campari	£0.33
15ml Aperol	£0.32
50ml blood orange juice	£0.08
50ml pink grapefruit juice	£0.05
15ml runny honey	£0.12
15ml lemon juice	£0.11
50ml soda water	£0.05
Blood orange	£0.15
Garnish	£0.03
Total:	**£1.77**

EQUIPMENT:
Scales
Spoon
Cocktail shaker
Hawthorne strainer

METHOD:
Add all ingredients (except soda) to your shaker, fill with cubed ice, shake and strain into wine glass filled with cubed ice.

SERVED IN:
Wine glass

ICE:
Cubed

GARNISH:
Pink grapefruit slice

 **JJ SAYS**

Whenever the sun drops out of sight, night falls, and for me that's when my naughty side detects trouble, and I'm ready to play up. The spritz is just that drink that captures the sun, but also the fun. Of course, we all have our favourite sunsets, the Italians have so many to choose from, but mine will always be Waterloo Bridge, with the Kinks in my headphones. I rarely find more peace in the hustle and bustle of this crazy city I'm proud to call home.

Original Recipe:

APEROL SPRITZ

★ 50ml Aperol
★ 75ml prosecco
★ 25ml soda water

Fill a wine glass two-thirds of the way with cubed ice, add all the ingredients, give a gentle stir and garnish with a wedge of orange.

History:

Created by the team at The Craft Cocktail Company in 2017 and inspired by our love of Italian aperitivos. The spritz is a wine and soda-based drink from north east Italy, in particular Venice. The name comes from the German word Spritzen, meaning spray or splash. The most famous versions are the Aperol Spritz and the Campari Spritz, on which the Americano is based, and regularly consumed around sunset, before dinner. All history aside, get to your kitchen and start mixing one of these babies up!

RAMOS GIN SILVER FIZZ

Lightly creamy, heavy on the gin, and with an elegant, long length, the Ramos Gin Fizz is simply stunning and ready for the red carpet. Feel free to sip with soda, but give the Champagne version a try, this classic deserves beautiful bubbles!

INGREDIENTS

50ml gin	£1.05
50ml Champagne	£1.30
30g egg white	£0.15
5ml orange flower water	£0.05
15ml lemon juice	£0.11
15ml double cream	£0.06
30ml sugar syrup	£0.03
3 drops vanilla extract	£0.06
Total:	**£2.81**

EQUIPMENT:
Scales
Spoon
Cocktail shaker
Blender (optional)

METHOD:
Shake. Add all the ingredients (except Champagne) to your shaker, shake for 1 full minute, strain into a chilled Collins glass, then gently top with Champagne. The key is to get a tall foamy head. Alternatively throw it all (except Champagne) in a blender with 1 cube of ice for 1 minute, then top with Champagne.

SERVED IN:
Collins glass

ICE:
Cubed

GARNISH:
None

Original Recipe:

RAMOS GIN FIZZ

- ★ 60ml gin
- ★ 15ml lime juice
- ★ 5ml orange flower water
- ★ 3 drops vanilla extract
- ★ 15ml egg white
- ★ Top soda water
- ★ 15ml lemon juice
- ★ 25ml sugar syrup
- ★ 30ml single cream

Add all the ingredients (except the soda) into a shaker, add ice and shake vigorously. Remove ice and dry shake for a whole minute. If you fancy the traditional method, when you suspect you're done shaking, think again. You've only just begun! A full 12 minutes of shaking is required. Strain into a chilled tall glass, carefully top with soda, and garnish with half a lemon slice and a mint sprig.

The "cocktail Oscars" are held in New Orleans every year, from where this drink was born. The city really doesn't sleep, and they love their heritage, of which is bountiful. Next time you go make sure you dance down Bourbon Street, unwind to the sounds of Louis Armstrong in the legendary jazz clubs, chomp on Creole classics while sat on steamboats slowly making their way down the Mississippi river. You're sure to fall in love with it as much as I have.

History:

A staple in New Orleans, the Ramos Gin Fizz was invented by Henry C. Ramos in 1888 at his bar 'The Imperial Cabinet Saloon'. It was originally called a New Orleans Fizz and was so popular Henry had to employ extra staff known as 'the shaker boys' who would be lined up along the bar shaking this delightful concoction to keep up with the demand.

CLOVER CLUB

Sweet and sour, dry and fruity, don't judge this drink by its colour. It's one of the best-selling drinks in London Cocktail Club history, and never off the menu for long. Now we've made it even easier to shake at home.

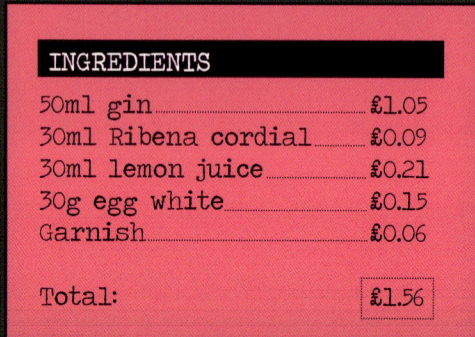

INGREDIENTS	
50ml gin	£1.05
30ml Ribena cordial	£0.09
30ml lemon juice	£0.21
30g egg white	£0.15
Garnish	£0.06
Total:	£1.56

EQUIPMENT:
Scales
Spoon
Cocktail shaker
Hawthorne strainer

METHOD:
Add all ingredients to your shaker, add cubed ice, shake and strain into chilled coupe glass.

SERVED IN:
Coupe glass

ICE:
None

GARNISH:
1 floating raspberry

There are a few drinks that I religiously order when I'm spoilt for choice and not 100 per cent ready to pick from the main menu in any great cocktail bar. Either a Tom Collins, a White Lady or a Clover Club will ready me before I jump in to something a little more adventurous. Often it's these same drinks that will be the true test of any great bartender or bar.

Original Recipe:

CLOVER CLUB (LOWE'S RECIPE)

★ 30ml gin
★ 30ml dry vermouth
★ 30ml lemon juice
★ 20ml raspberry syrup
★ 15ml egg white

Shaken into a coupe glass. Garnish with a fresh raspberry.

History:

Drinks historians date The Clover Club back to the 1909 book, Drinks - How to Mix and Serve, by Paul E. Lowe. It was created at the Bellevue-Stratford in Philadelphia, the city's most fashionable hotel at the time, where The Clover Club, an elite all-male club whose members were top lawyers and writers, met regularly. Work hard, play harder we say!

ROSE PETAL MARTINI

Light, crisp and dry, you won't need to travel to the south of France for a true taste of Provence, so close your eyes and picture of the Côte d'Azur with each and every sip.

INGREDIENTS

40ml gin	£0.84
40ml cranberry juice	£0.04
15ml rose petal water	£0.14
20ml sugar syrup*	£0.02
20ml lemon juice	£0.14
Garnish	£0.03
Total:	**£1.21**

★ In a saucepan add 500ml caster sugar to 500ml of hot water from the kettle, gently simmer until all the sugar has dissolved and the syrup is clear. Let it cool, then pour into an empty bottle and refrigerate (lasts up to 6 weeks).

EQUIPMENT:
Scales
Cocktail shaker
Hawthorne strainer
Tea strainer

METHOD:
Add all ingredients to your shaker, add cubed ice, shake and fine strain into chilled martini glass.

SERVED IN:
Martini glass

ICE:
None

GARNISH:
A rose petal

I created this cocktail back in 2010 with LCC legend Lee Ottery. The number one fan of this twisted cosmopolitan is none other than my culinary mentor Raymond Blanc! Since his first sip, he's ordered one every time he is in one of our London Cocktail Clubs, and if that's not endorsement enough then try mixing one up yourself, I'm sure you'll be hooked for life just like he is!

Original Recipe:
ROSE WATER JULAB

★ 50ml Kentucky bourbon
★ 6-8 mint leaves
★ 6 drops of rose water
★ 1 tbsp brown sugar

Add the mint leaves, rose water and brown sugar to a julep tin. Lightly press the ingredients with a muddler, fill two-thirds with crushed ice, add bourbon, churn, and then cap with crushed ice. Garnish with a mint sprig and rose petal.

History:

The word julep is Persian for rose water, and this meaning has been traced back to an old Arabic drink called a Julab, which was made with rose petals and water, and believed to have medicinal benefits. The drink travelled from the middle east to the Mediterranean where the rose petals were cast aside for the more accessible mint leaves. Eventually the drink made its way over to the United States in the early 19th century where Senator Henry Clay of Kentucky introduced it to friends at the Round Robin Bar at the Willard Hotel in Washington DC. The Americans added their beloved bourbon and the rest as they say, is history!

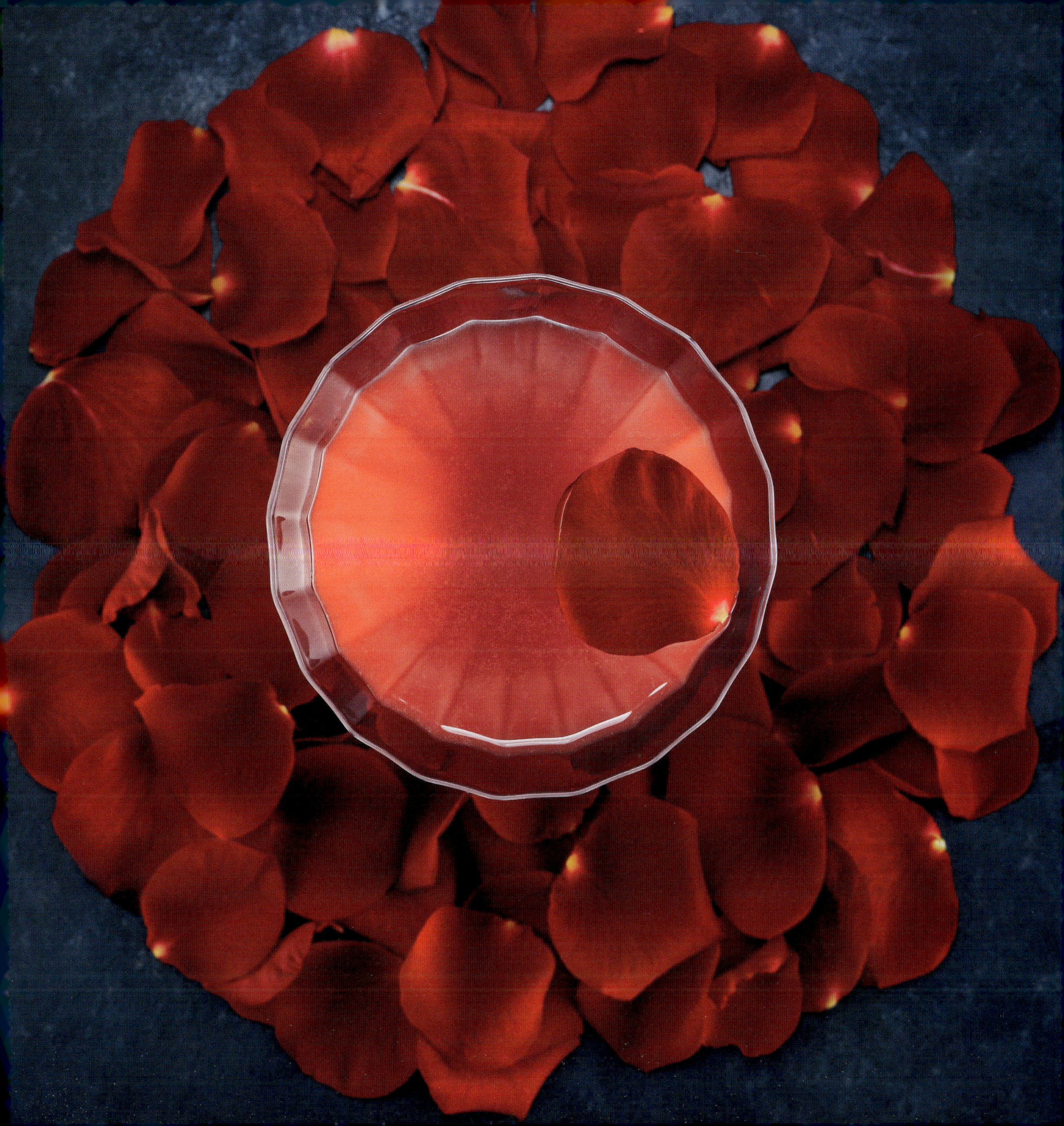

7-9PM

"Put away your corkscrew and dispense with your bottle opener. Cocktails are the future of over-dinner drinks. Matching ingredients is a passion of mine and with my experience of working in kitchens there is a plethora of potential possibilities you can mix with your drinks that'll bring the dining experience to life. Close your eyes and transport yourself on rainy days back to the Caribbean while sipping a Mai Tai between mouthfuls of jerk chicken. You'll practically feel the sun on your face and sand between your toes. All from your cosy cul-de-sac without a dent in the wallet."

DINNER

SIDECAR

Paris has produced some legendary classic cocktails, and the Sidecar is one of the most recognisable in the world to date. Crunch on the sugar granules from the rim for little bursts of sweetness as you gulp down this sour, earthy, gem of a drink.

INGREDIENTS	
40ml Cognac	£0.96
20ml Triple Sec	£0.36
20ml lemon juice	£0.14
10ml sugar syrup*	£0.01
2 dashes Angostura bitters	£0.10
Garnish	£0.07
Total:	**£1.64**

EQUIPMENT:
Scales
Spoon
Cocktail shaker
Hawthorne strainer

METHOD:
Shake. Add all ingredients to your shaker, shake and strain into a chilled vintage wine glass filled with cubed ice.

SERVED IN:
Vintage wine glass

ICE:
Cubed

GARNISH:
Sugar rim (moisten outside of rim with lemon and gently coat in fine sugar)
Orange twist

★ In a saucepan add 500ml caster sugar to 500ml of hot water from the kettle, gently simmer until all the sugar has dissolved and the syrup is clear. Let it cool, then pour into an empty bottle and refrigerate (lasts up to 6 weeks).

Food for thought... I adore Paris as much as anyone, the bar scene there is constantly evolving, as are the many tastes and flavours of one of the world's most creative cities. As this drink is a French native, I've chosen a food dish with just as much heritage - garlic butter Escargot ideally with flambé pastis! The Sidecar's acidity will of course cut through the garlic butter, but the anise flavour from the flambé would finish off a match made in heaven!

Original Recipe:

BRANDY CRUSTA

★ 50ml Cognac
★ 7.5ml Triple Sec liqueur
★ 7.5ml maraschino liqueur
★ 15ml lemon juice
★ 10ml sugar syrup
★ 2 dashes Angostura bitters

Shake and strain into chilled cocktail glass with a sugar rim (moisten outside of rim with lemon and gently coat in fine sugar), and garnish with a twist of lemon.

History:

The history of the Sidecar is once again, a disputed one. One story in particular seems to crop up frequently that the Sidecar was created in 1933 in Harry's Bar, Paris, for an American army captain who enjoyed cruising around in a motorcycle sidecar, presumably while wearing aviator goggles and muttering Hemingway-esque quips. The image of that alone is worth a giggle.

BRAMBLE

Tall, refreshing and fruity! The berry flavours here are light, but distinctive, allowing the gin to be the star of the show. I'd have a Bramble over a gin and tonic any day!

INGREDIENTS

50ml gin	£1.05
20ml lemon juice	£0.14
10ml sugar syrup*	£0.01
20ml Ribena cordial	£0.06
Garnish	£0.09
Total:	£1.35

★ In a saucepan add 500ml caster sugar to 500ml of hot water from the kettle, gently simmer until all the sugar has dissolved and the syrup is clear. Let it cool, then pour into an empty bottle and refrigerate (lasts up to 6 weeks).

EQUIPMENT:
Scales
Spoon

METHOD:
Build. Add the first three ingredients to your Collins glass, stir, then gently pour Ribena cordial over the top of the drink.

SERVED IN:
Collins glass

ICE:
Cubed

GARNISH:
Lemon slice
Mint sprig

Food for thought... Since I was a kid I've always loved a Chinese takeaway in front of the TV on a Sunday night. The one dish you could never be without was duck and pancakes of course, smeared with plum sauce and built up with batons of juicy cucumber and crunchy spring onion. The bramble is the perfect companion, with the plum and dark fruits going hand in hand, plus the seasoning being uplifted by the botanicals in the gin.

Original Recipe:

BRAMBLE

- ★ 30ml gin
- ★ 20ml lemon juice
- ★ 15ml sugar syrup
- ★ 20ml crème de mure/blackberry liqueur

Add all ingredients (except crème de mure) to a shaker, add ice and shake. Strain into a large rocks glass filled with crushed ice. Pour crème de mure over ice for 'bleeding effect'. Garnish with half a lemon slice and a blackberry.

History:

A bramble is the bush that blackberries grow on, hence the liquor required to mix this modern day classic. The bramble was created in the 1980s by legendary London bartender Dick Bradsell whilst working at Fred's Club in Soho. He initially wanted to invent a truly British drink, though he could not source an acceptable British crème de mure and lemons are not exactly native to the UK, but a beautiful accident was created, and a legend was born.

SWIZZLE MY TIE

The Mai Tai is one of the most loved drinks in the world, most probably for complex flavour, yet simple structure. The sweetness of the orgeat (almond and rose petal syrup) with rum and citrus balances perfectly every time.

INGREDIENTS

25ml white rum	£0.53
25ml dark rum	£0.50
25ml lime juice	£0.25
20ml demerara syrup*	£0.04
25ml pineapple juice	£0.03
5ml almond extract	£0.10
1 dash Angostura bitters	£0.05
Garnish	£0.07
Total:	**£1.57**

★ In a saucepan add 100ml demerara sugar to 100ml of hot water from the kettle, gently simmer until all the sugar has dissolved. Let it cool, then pour into an empty bottle and refrigerate (lasts up to 6 weeks).

Original Recipe:

MAI TAI (TRADER VIC'S)

- ★ 25ml white rum (preferably Martinique)
- ★ 25ml dark rum (preferably Jamaican)
- ★ 25ml lime juice
- ★ 15ml orange curaçao
- ★ 15ml almond syrup

Shake all ingredients, then strain into a rocks glass filled with crushed ice. Garnish with a lime wedge and mint sprig.

EQUIPMENT:
Scales
Cocktail shaker
Hawthorne strainer

METHOD:
Add all ingredients to a shaker, add cubed ice, shake and strain into a rocks glass or tiki cup filled with cubed ice.

SERVED IN:
Tiki Mug

ICE:
Cubed

GARNISH:
Mint sprig
Orange slice
Grated nutmeg

Food for thought... I love a splash of pineapple in my Mai Tais. In fact I love a splash of pineapple in just about everything! You guessed it, my food pairing for this little legend is Hawaiian pizza! I have no idea why pineapple on pizza is so controversial, I love it, in fact I rarely eat pizza without it. Biting in to hot juicy grilled pineapple on a pizza or in a burger is the dream meal after a long day's surfing at the beach.

History:

The Mai Tai came to life in 1944 and is the masterpiece of Tiki god Victor Bergeron, better known as Trader Vic. The story goes, a guest at his famed Trader Vic's restaurant in Oakland, California took a first sip and exclaimed "Maitai roa ae!", which is Tahitian for "Out of this world!" His original recipe used a 17-year aged Wray and Nephew rum from Jamaica. The few remaining bottles of this rum have been sold at auctions for over $50,000. Better start saving those pennies!

SHRUB

"Vinegar in a cocktail... are you mad?!", well yes, I am a little, but not when it comes to this cool concoction. Sweetness from balsamic and length from the ginger make it refreshing and aromatic at the same time.

INGREDIENTS	
25ml aged rum	£0.90
100ml ginger ale	£0.10
25ml pomegranate molasses	£0.40
10ml balsamic vinegar	£0.08
Garnish: Baby's Breath or your choice of edible flower	£0.10
Total:	**£1.58**

EQUIPMENT:
Scales
Spoon
Cocktail shaker
Hawthorne strainer
Fine strainer

METHOD:
Shake. Add all ingredients to your shaker, fill with cubed ice, shake and fine strain into chilled flute.

SERVED IN:
Flute glass

ICE:
None

GARNISH:
Your choice of edible flower

Food for thought... There's only one classic Friday filler that is ideal for a vinegar-flavoured flute and that is fish and chips! Ginger pairs with the batter, and with balsamic and its less sexy cousin, malt vinegar, there's so many crossovers that are so easy to see why they work. Be careful when mixing with vinegar as shrubs are either very right or very wrong. The drink's smell will often be the deciding factor.

Original Recipe:

MEDICINAL CORDIAL

★ 1 tbsp dandelion root
★ 1 tbsp burdock root
★ 20g fresh ginger root
★ 1 star anise
★ 300ml water
★ 300g dark brown sugar

Simmer all ingredients in a pan for 10 minutes, let it cool, strain, bottle and refrigerate. The combination of dandelion and burdock is great for cleansing the liver, and you can add this cordial to alcoholic and non-alcoholic cocktails.

History:

Medicinal cordials made in 15th century England are believed to have been the starting point for shrubs. Typically made with brandy or rum, sugar and citrus fruit, the drink became popular with English smugglers in the 1680s who were trying to avoid paying import taxes on their shipped goods. The cheeky little buggers would sink barrels of spirits off-shore, then smuggle them in under the cover of darkness. Adding fruit flavours masked the taste of seawater. By the 17th century vinegar was often used as an alternative to citrus juices in the preservation of berries and other fruits for the off-season, which gives us the flavour profile that we know as a shrub to this day.

MANGO LASSI

Sweet and spicy, this creamy cooling concoction is designed to take the heat out of your food on a hot day while adding some fruity flavour. Once you've finished it, you'll be left wanting more.

INGREDIENTS	
45ml Scotch whisky	£0.95
180g fresh mango	£1.26
125ml low fat yoghurt	£0.38
25ml runny honey	£0.20
2 cardamom pods (whole)	£0.01
10g pistachios	£0.12
Garnish	£0.30
Total:	**£3.22**

EQUIPMENT:
Scales
Blender
Mixing spoon

METHOD:
Blend. Add all ingredients to your blender with five ice cubes and blend until smooth.

SERVED IN:
Collins glass

ICE:
None

GARNISH:
Saffron (if you're feeling fancy)
2 crumbled pistachios

 **SAYS**

Food for thought... My long-lasting love of Indian food comes from growing up in Birmingham where some of the world's best curries come from. To pair this lassi I'm going for a full-on sugar rush by adding some coconut to the mango flavours and recommending a classic creamy Korma. Throw in some Peshwari naan to indulge yourself to death, we all deserve at least one cheat day a week!

Original Recipe:

LASSI (TRADITIONAL RECIPE)

★ 300ml plain natural yoghurt
★ 200ml water
★ 2 tsp white sugar
★ Pinch salt

Blend all the ingredients until smooth and creamy, then pour into a tall glass.

History:

This delicious yoghurt-based drink is originally from the lands of Punjab and Multan in Northern India to cool the effect of hot summers. Lassi can be referred to as an 'ancient smoothie' and indeed the first yoghurt smoothie in the world. The concept originated somewhere around 1000 BC! It is well known for giving a calming effect to the stomach and mind too, so knock a few back with a clear conscience.

SHERRY COBBLER

The perfect combination of sexy and cute. I love this drink's elegance, with a touch of fruity fun. Not all pineapple flavours have to be served in Tiki cups, and this is a perfect example why.

INGREDIENTS

60ml sherry	£1.02
6 mint leaves	£0.04
20ml orange juice	£0.02
20ml pineapple juice	£0.02
20ml sugar syrup*	£0.02
2 raspberries	£0.12
10ml lemon juice	£0.07
Garnish	£0.53
Total:	**£1.84**

★ In a saucepan add 500ml caster sugar to 500ml of hot water from the kettle, gently simmer until all the sugar has dissolved and the syrup is clear. Let it cool, then pour into an empty bottle and refrigerate (lasts up to 6 weeks).

EQUIPMENT:
Scales
Cocktail shaker
Hawthorne strainer
Tea strainer

METHOD:
Add all ingredients to your shaker, add cubed ice, shake and fine strain into a chilled wine goblet.

SERVED IN:
Wine goblet

ICE:
Cubed

GARNISH:
Orange slice
Mint sprig
Lime slice
2 raspberries
2 red grapes
2 blueberries

Food for thought... A massive bowl of steamed mussels would make my eyes light up when placed next to a sherry cobbler! The fruity yet dry flavours in the cocktail would undoubtedly wash back the tiny chewy morsels of goodness already cooked in a classic, aromatic, wine reduction. Sherry is a brilliant base to mix with, as its low alcohol content doesn't take away from its powerful taste.

Original Recipe:

SHERRY COBBLER

★ 75ml sherry (medium dry)
★ 1 tbsp superfine sugar
★ 3 slices of orange

Muddle orange slices and sugar in bottom of Boston tin. Add cubed ice, shake and strain into Collins glass filled with crushed ice. Garnish with seasonal berries and a sprig of mint.

History:

This cocktail was invented in America in the 1800s, when British merchants were able to import sherry for the first time. By the end of the 1930s this wine-based cocktail dominated America. Some clever so-and-so combined it with the biggest novelty of the day - ice. In addition to the ice, the first straws (usually made from straw or hollow pasta) had been invented and were used for the first time in this cocktail, slurp, slurp!

EARL GREY SOUR

This quintessential cuppa is simply stunning. Earl Grey tea is infused with bergamot citrus fruit to give it its famous lasting taste and smell. We've added a glug of gin and a smack of citrus to really bring it alive!

INGREDIENTS

50ml gin	£1.05
20ml lemon juice	£0.14
30g egg white	£0.15
20ml Earl Grey tea syrup*	£0.06
Garnish	£0.05
Total:	£1.45

★ Earl Grey tea syrup: In a saucepan add one tea bag for every 100ml of sugar syrup. Simmer on a medium heat for 6 minutes. Let the mixture cool, remove tea bags, pour into a bottle or kilner jar and refrigerate (lasts up to 6 weeks).

EQUIPMENT:
Scales
Spoon
Cocktail shaker
Hawthorne strainer

METHOD:
Shake. Add all the ingredients to your shaker, fill with cubed ice, shake and strain into a tea cup.

SERVED IN:
Tea cup

ICE:
None

GARNISH:
Lemon twist

Food for thought... The food pairing here was a foregone conclusion, it HAS to be afternoon tea. I love the tinkering of teacups on saucers, sampling crust-less cucumber finger sandwiches, all while debating if jam should go on your scone before or after the cream (before, the Queen says so). Though I prefer Champagne with my afternoon tea to tea alone, the Earl Grey Sour clearly trumps them both.

History:
Our Early Grey Sour is based on the White Lady, also referred to as a Chelsea Sidecar or Delilah. Believed to have been created by Harry MacElhone in 1919, his recipe originally called for crème de menthe instead of gin, though he allegedly switched to the junipery goodness that is gin in 1929 when he moved to Harry's New York Bar in Paris.

Original Recipe:
WHITE LADY
★ 40ml gin
★ 20ml Cointreau
★ 20ml lemon juice
★ 15ml egg white
★ 5ml sugar syrup (optional)

Dry shake then shake with ice before serving into a coupe glass. Garnish with a lemon twist.

CLARET PUNCH

Mixing with wines is easy, and this grown-up tipple exemplifies just that. Cheaper wines come alive with just a few adjustments, making this red wine-based drink more accessible in the summer, and for lighter, more delicate foods.

INGREDIENTS	
25ml brandy	£0.65
25ml Grand Marnier	£0.93
100ml red wine	£1.20
20ml lemon juice	£0.14
20ml sugar syrup*	£0.02
50ml soda	£0.05
Garnish	£0.02
Total:	£3.01

EQUIPMENT:
Scales
Spoon

METHOD:
Build. Add all ingredients (except soda) to a large wine goblet, add cubed ice, stir, and then top with soda. Feel free to multiply this recipe and serve in a large water jug or similar.

SERVED IN:
Large wine goblet

ICE:
Cubed

GARNISH:
Mint sprig

★ In a saucepan add 500ml caster sugar to 500ml of hot water from the kettle, gently simmer until all the sugar has dissolved and the syrup is clear. Let it cool, then pour into an empty bottle and refrigerate (lasts up to 6 weeks).

Original Recipe:

CLARET CUP PUNCH

★ 100ml claret/Bordeaux wine
★ 50ml brandy
★ 25ml curaçao
★ 50ml soda water
★ 2 tbsp sugar
★ 1 handful of seasonal fruits

Add all ingredients to a claret cup and stir. Traditionally ice would not have been available, but we would suggest using ice. Garnish with Borage, strawberries and grapes.

Food for thought… My food pairing here would have to be Lancashire hot pot, or any similar rich and meaty stews. My mom grew up in Preston, Lancashire, so I've had my fair share. A refreshing punch would be my ideal partner to wash it down. Though it may be lighter in body than a red wine, the brandy and Grand Marnier will add a bloody finish that will pair well with any red meat dishes.

History:

The Claret Punch, which is a relative of Sangria, was very popular in the 1800s, and was often served at parties. Every posh Georgian household or even Royal wedding had its own recipe for 'the best Claret Cup'. The basic recipe is red wine, lemon, sugar and carbonated water. To that simple and inexpensive mix, you can add anything you want.

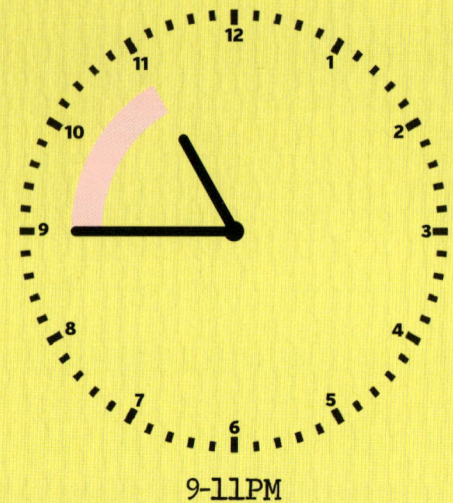

9-11PM

"Don't bother dishing up dessert, this diverse list of indulgent drinks is guaranteed to make you smile. Willy Wonka himself would have struggled to cultivate these contemporary creamy concoctions. Forget about the carbs, each sip is worth every calorie. No great story started with a salad, so boot up your blender and get mixing... you can thank me later!"

PUDDING

ANGEL DELIGHT FLIP

Giggle with delight to this creamy, mouth-filling and foamy, frothy flip! Nostalgia in a glass, topped with a toasted marshmallow for good measure, you'll be sure to inhale a few of these in quick succession, but which flavour will you choose?

INGREDIENTS

20ml vodka	£0.20
40ml Baileys	£0.86
1 whole egg	£0.15
4 tsp Angel Delight (strawberry flavour) powder	£0.14
25ml double cream	£0.09
25ml milk	£0.01
Garnish	£0.04
Total:	**£1.49**

EQUIPMENT:
Scales
Spoon
Cocktail shaker
Hawthorne strainer
Blow torch

METHOD:
Shake. Add all ingredients to your shaker, add cubed ice, shake and strain into a chilled martini glass.

SERVED IN:
Martini glass

ICE:
None

GARNISH:
Toasted marshmallow (using blow torch)

 **JL SAYS**
As a kid, I'd squeal with joy when mom took the packet of instant mousse mix out of the cupboard. My sister Ava and I would fight over who got to lick the whisk or the bowl, and waiting 15 minutes for it to rise in the fridge felt like 3 hours (I was still convinced it was overnight till I read the packet recently). The repetitive prodding and nagging of "mom is it done yet?!" must have made her want to jump out the window.

Original Recipe:

POSSET (TRADITIONAL RECIPE)

★ 1 egg
★ 30g caster sugar
★ 100ml double cream
★ 50ml dark ale
★ Pinch of nutmeg

Whisk the cream and eggs into a saucepan and heat gently. Once warm, whisk in the sugar until dissolved, then add the beer and nutmeg. Continue to cook on high until the mixture forms a layer of egg and curd on top, then pour into a mug.

History:

Believed to have originated somewhere in 15th century England, the posset is the predecessor to Eggnog. It was a peasant drink often used as a cold and flu remedy. Food at that time was scarce, so egg and cream were added to wine or ale, a little spice, then the mixture was heated in an attempt to pasteurise it which results in the top layer becoming a textured eggy curd. Sounds delish!

BANOFFEE SUNDAE

Whose mouth doesn't water at the idea of sinking your fork in to a chunky slice of banoffee pie!? This cocktail is beyond delicious, with the classic toffee, banana and cream melting together in perfect harmony!

INGREDIENTS

25ml amaretto	£0.54
25ml toffee vodka	£0.50
2 tsp Nesquik	£0.06
3 tsp peanut butter	£0.04
2 scoops (65g per scoop) vanilla ice cream	£0.06
30ml butterscotch sauce	£0.05
50ml milk	£0.02
Garnish	£0.25
Total:	£1.52

EQUIPMENT:
Scales
Spoon
Blender

METHOD:
Blend. Add all ingredients to your blender with two ice cubes and blend until smooth.

SERVED IN:
Sundae glass

ICE:
None

GARNISH:
Whipped UHT cream
Chopped nuts
Chocolate sauce
Banana sweets
Banana dolphin

 I've been meaning to write this drink for YEARS! So, when condensing my list of eight favourite puddings from 30 for this chapter, I found my chance! I love bananas, and I'm that freak who prefers banana milkshakes in fast food restaurants (if the machine ever works). Banana ice cream is a blessing, and even banana bread beats any loaf on the planet for me. I threw in some peanut butter for good measure, so I hope you really enjoy it as much as I do.

Original Recipe:

DIRTY BANANA

★ 40ml white rum
★ 25ml Kahlúa
★ 25ml banana liqueur
★ 25ml single cream
★ 25ml milk
★ 1 ripe banana

Add all ingredients to a blender with a handful of crushed ice, blend, and then pour into a tall glass. Serve with a long straw.

History:

We drew inspiration for our Banoffee Sundae from a Jamaican staple, the Dirty Banana, which is far more delicious than its name would lead you to believe. Like so many cocktails, its creator and exact origins are unknown. This blended drink gets its "dirty" reputation from a hit of Kahlúa and aged rum, along with a ripe banana and cream, that affect the colour. It's like a boozy banana split served in a tall glass. If that hasn't sold it to you, we don't know what will.

ETON MESS

Cricket bats at the ready, we're off for a jolly good "knock-a-back"! This cheeky in-swinger calls for a feather of gin, full toss of strawberry, cutter of cream, and beamer of Baileys... now howzat for a decent innings?!

INGREDIENTS

25ml gin	£0.50
25ml Baileys	£0.54
30g egg white	£0.15
30g strawberry jam	£0.13
15ml lemon juice	£0.06
15ml double cream	£0.06
3 drops vanilla extract (optional)	£0.06
Garnish	£0.02
Total:	**£1.52**

EQUIPMENT:
Scales
Spoon
Cocktail shaker
Hawthorne strainer
Tea strainer

METHOD:
Shake. Add all ingredients to your shaker, add cubed ice, shake and fine strain into a chilled martini glass.

SERVED IN:
Martini glass

ICE:
None

GARNISH:
Half a strawberry

You don't have to be "taking lunch" to enjoy an Eton Mess, though some rituals work for good reason. Though the mess was born in Berkshire, strawberries and cream in fact comes from my home town of Birmingham. The Edgbaston Archery and Lawn Tennis Society, founded in the 1860s, is the oldest in the country, and was in fact in a strawberry field, hence its relationship with tennis lovers worldwide. I'd argue that my incarnation is even better!

Original Recipe:

STRAWBERRY SHORTCAKE (TGI FRIDAYS)

★ 40ml amaretto
★ 60ml milk
★ 60g frozen (thawed) strawberries
★ 2 scoops vanilla ice cream

Add all ingredients to a blender with a handful of crushed ice, blend for 30 seconds, then pour into a tall glass. Garnish with whipped cream and a fresh strawberry on the rim.

History:

We are not suggesting you serve it this way, but the generally-accepted story is that the strawberry, meringue and cream pudding was dropped on the floor at an Eton v Harrow cricket match in the late 19th century. Instead of wasting the food, it was simply scooped up off the floor and served. Remember to take a packed lunch whenever attending an Eton cricket match.

APPLE & BLACKBERRY CRUMBLE

School lunches were a thing of beauty when humble crumble made the menu. Stodgy, crispy, but full of flavour! I've taken out the stodge and put in some spiced rum to make this pudding punch above its weight.

INGREDIENTS	
50ml spiced rum	£0.50
3 drops vanilla extract	£0.06
50ml custard (from a carton)	£0.13
50ml apple juice	£0.05
4 blackberries	£0.14
Pinch cinnamon	£0.02
1 whole egg	£0.15
10ml demerara syrup*	£0.02
Garnish	£0.12
Total:	**£1.19**

EQUIPMENT:
Scales
Spoon
Cocktail shaker
Hawthorne strainer

METHOD:
Shake. Add all ingredients to your shaker, add cubed ice, shake and strain into a rocks glass filled with cubed ice

SERVED IN:
Rocks glass

ICE:
Cubed

GARNISH:
Crumble
1 tsp cinnamon
1 tbsp brown sugar
1 tbsp custard
1 blackberry
Mint sprig

I met Leigh Miller and Steve Locke (owners of the Be At One cocktail bars) at one of my very first cocktail competitions at Prohibition Bar in Liverpool 2004. I made this drink for them then, though I decided to "layer" the custard, which instantly fell to the bottom of the glass in a mess! I was so embarrassed, but they graciously tasted it anyway. I didn't win the competition of course, but I did win the chance to work for them a year later, my first and most memorable job I had in London. Their passion for training and great service is still ingrained in me today.

★ In a saucepan add 100ml demerara sugar to 100ml of hot water from the kettle, gently simmer until all the sugar has dissolved. Let it cool, then pour into an empty bottle and refrigerate (lasts up to 6 weeks).

History:

Becoming popular in the early 20th century, the Brandy Alexander is widely known for having been John Lennon's favourite drink. It's a variation of an earlier cocktail called an 'Alexander' which used gin instead of the now popular brandy, everything else remains the same. Although there are a few stories regarding the inception of this fabulous drink, it was likely named after Troy Alexander, a bartender at Rector's, a New York City restaurant, who created the drink in order to serve a white drink at a dinner celebrating Phoebe Snow, a character in a popular advertising campaign.

Original Recipe:
BRANDY ALEXANDER

★ 30ml Cognac
★ 30ml crème de cacao (white)
★ 30ml single cream

Add all ingredients to a shaker, add ice, shake and strain into a chilled martini glass. Garnish with grated nutmeg.

THE CUPTAIL

Cupcakes and cocktails are a match made in heaven, so why not mix them together?! Well, I did, and this creamy, nutty, vanilla number is sure to put a smile on your face even on a rainy day!

INGREDIENTS	
25ml amaretto	£0.54
25ml Baileys	£0.54
5ml sugar syrup*	£0.01
3 drops vanilla extract	£0.06
1 whole egg	£0.15
Garnish	£0.08
Total:	£1.38

★ In a saucepan add 500ml caster sugar to 500ml of hot water from the kettle, gently simmer until all the sugar has dissolved and the syrup is clear. Let it cool, then pour into an empty bottle and refrigerate (lasts up to 6 weeks).

EQUIPMENT:
Scales
Cocktail shaker
Hawthorne strainer

METHOD:
Add all ingredients to your shaker, add cubed ice, shake and strain into a rocks glass filled with cubed ice.

SERVED IN:
Rocks glass

ICE:
Cubed

GARNISH:
Squirty cream
100s & 1000s sprinkles
Cherry

This was a wicked collaboration with "Mychelles Baketique" way back in 2011. Michelle was teaching cake decoration and I was teaching a mixology class on "cuptails" in an attempt to do a boozy afternoon tea. Needless to say, the sessions went down a storm (literally, there was mess everywhere!), and the Cuptail found its way on to the LCC menu where I insisted it be topped with vanilla frosting and sprinkles. My bartenders never forgave me for that garnish, so trust me when I say the squirty cream is A LOT easier to finish this off!

Original Recipe:

SHERRY FLIP

★ 60ml cream sherry
★ 15ml sugar
★ 15ml single cream
★ 1 whole egg

Shake all ingredients and strain into a chilled small wine goblet. Garnish with some grated nutmeg.

History:

The term 'Flip' was first used in 1695 to describe a mixture of beer, rum, and sugar. Considered a sailor's drink in England, the ingredients were usually poured back and forth between two mugs to combine, and then heated on a stove. In colonial taverns they were stirred with a red-hot iron rod (known as a loggerhead) that had been heated in the fireplace. This warmed and frothed (or "flipped") the mixture, which inspired the name.

CHOCOLATE HARDSHAKE

Calling all chocoholics... Surely this is your Utopia in a glass? Chocolate milk, chocolate ice cream and chocolate sauce - it's all going down (with a hit of vodka and Baileys) in this take on the classic Mudslide.

INGREDIENTS	
25ml vodka	£0.50
25ml Baileys	£0.54
25ml chocolate sauce	£0.15
50ml milk	£0.02
2 scoops (65g per scoop) chocolate ice cream	£0.06
Garnish	£0.30
Total:	£1.57

EQUIPMENT:
Scales
Spoon
Cocktail shaker
Hawthorne strainer

METHOD:
Add all ingredients to your shaker, add cubed ice, shake and strain into a Collins glass.

SERVED IN:
Collins glass

ICE:
None

GARNISH:
Chocolate mini egg
3 Maltesers
Squirty cream
Chocolate 100s & 1000s
Cherry
Condensed milk rim
(Dip the rim of the glass in condensed milk and let it drip all down the side)

JL SAYS

This one goes out to my chocolate-loving brothers and sisters! My favourite chocolates of all time have to be Ferrero Rocher at home with a glass of red wine (yes I do love wine too). On the run I love a Cadbury's Picnic Bar, and at Christmas it would have to be a milk chocolate hazelnut with caramel from the legends at Quality Street, also known as THE PURPLE ONE! Whatever yours are and why, I'm sure you'll get stuck into this with no hesitation, though sip slow to avoid the brain freeze, if you can!

Original Recipe:
MUDSLIDE (WRECK BAR RECIPE)
★ 30ml vodka
★ 30ml Baileys
★ 30ml coffee liqueur

Add all ingredients to a blender with a cup of crushed ice, blend until smooth. Pour into a Collins glass and garnish with a brandied cherry and grated cinnamon.

History:

The Mudslide was very popular in the USA during the 1980s, however its origins can be traced back to the 1970s where it was allegedly invented at the Rum Points club, Wreck Bar and Grill on Grand Cayman in the Cayman Islands. Supposedly the drink was made out of necessity when the bartender was asked to make a white Russian but had ran out of cream, so he used Baileys instead.

COOKIES & CREAM

Movie lovers out there are going to scream for this star-studded mash-up of all our favourite "confectionaries". Next time you lock yourself in the house for a movie marathon, close the curtains, blend up this bad boy, sit back and relax, you're worth it.

INGREDIENTS

30ml bourbon whiskey	£0.60
30ml Baileys	£0.65
2 scoops (65g per scoop) vanilla ice cream	£0.06
4 small chocolate chip cookies	£0.32
Handful of popcorn	£0.10
Garnish	£0.12
Total:	**£1.85**

EQUIPMENT:
Scales
Blender

METHOD:
Blend. Add all ingredients to your blender with two ice cubes and blend until smooth.

SERVED IN:
Handled jar

ICE:
None

GARNISH:
Handful of sweet popcorn
3 Maltesers
1 chocolate chip cookie

 I love to head to the cinema for a screening. The excitement hasn't gone away as I've gotten older, so I've paid homage with the ultimate cinema smoothies. I love the texture on this cocktail so blend for about 10 seconds and have a look at how many chunky bits you can handle. If you prefer it smooth then leave out the popcorn, if you like it super thick, then leave out the straw. Either way, make sure you buy way too many chocolates for your garnish, there's nothing worse than running out before the film's finished!

Original Recipe:

SCREAMING ORGASM

- ★ 25ml vodka
- ★ 25ml Kahlúa
- ★ 25ml amaretto
- ★ 25ml Baileys
- ★ 25ml single cream
- ★ 25ml milk

Add all ingredients to shaker, add ice, shake and strain into tall glass filled with crushed ice. Garnish with grated chocolate or chocolate powder.

History:

Despite the controversial name which made the drink very popular in the 1980s, very little is known about this sexy little number. The original version, which has no vodka, is known simply as an 'orgasm'. Add the vodka and it becomes a 'screaming orgasm'. Tom Cruise famously mentions this drink whilst performing his last bartender poet speech during the 1988 film 'Cocktail'. Maybe Tom created it, you never know.

ESPRESSO MARTINI

This post-meal pick-up is guaranteed to be a fave for almost every cocktail connoisseur. We've made it super speedy to shake this drink up for a rich coffee taste, with perfect foam, every time.

INGREDIENTS

40ml vodka	£0.80
20ml runny honey	£0.17
1 tsp instant coffee	£0.02
1 tsp Bournville chocolate powder	£0.01
50ml spring water	£0.05
Garnish	£0.02
Total:	£1.07

EQUIPMENT:
Scales
Spoon
Cocktail shaker
Hawthorne strainer

METHOD:
Shake. Add all ingredients to your shaker, add cubed ice, shake and strain into a chilled martini glass.

SERVED IN:
Martini glass

ICE:
None

GARNISH:
1 Bourbon biscuit

JJ SAYS
When I first opened London Cocktail Club I couldn't afford a coffee machine to make fresh espresso, in fact we couldn't afford ice wells behind the bar. So, I did what I had to and reached for the instant, carefully crafting a cocktail that become known as one of the best in the country. I've kept the secret as long as I can, but it's the process of freeze drying the coffee that makes it instant. It also gives the powder much more protein, which in turn makes our espresso martinis get their perfect "head" every time.

Original Recipe:
ESPRESSO MARTINI

★ 30ml vodka
★ 15ml Kahlúa
★ 15ml Tia Vodka
★ 25ml espresso
★ 10ml sugar syrup

The key is a fresh shot of espresso. Add all ingredients to your shaker, add ice, shake and strain into a chilled martini glass. Garnish with three coffee beans placed on the foam.

History:
It's the early 1980s, a famous female model walks into a bar in Soho and asks for a drink that will not only "wake me up, but f @k me up". That's exactly what happened to London bartender Dick Bradsell whilst working at the Soho Brasserie. So he reached for the nearby espresso machine, grabbed his favourite vodka and created this modern day classic which we all love. Pssst…the famous model was Kate Moss!

11PM-3AM

"This book is littered with cocktails that will get your night off to a great start, but through all my years of bartending, I can assure you that these marvellously mischievous martinis are guaranteed to galvanise girls and guys alike.

CAUTION!!! Side-effects may include; swinging on lampshades, singing your lungs out, dancing on tables until your heart's content and in extreme cases; texting your EX. Don't say I didn't warn you!"

HEISENBERG

Break out your beakers because it's about to get BAD. Since Walter White stepped out on our screens we've been geeking out on this crystal blue concoction. Stain your salts, and serve this head-spinner to your crew this weekend.

INGREDIENTS

50ml 100% agave tequila	£1.40
15ml agave syrup	£0.15
25ml lime juice	£0.15
3 drops blue food colouring	£0.02
Garnish	£0.15
Total:	**£1.87**

EQUIPMENT:
Scales
Cocktail shaker
Hawthorne strainer

METHOD:
Shake. Add all ingredients to your shaker, add cubed ice, shake and strain into a chemical beaker filled with cubed ice.

SERVED IN:
Chemical beaker

ICE:
Cubed

GARNISH:
Mini zip-lock baggie
1 tbsp rock salt
½ tsp blue food colouring (mix the salt and food colouring and insert into mini baggie)

 This has always been a fun drink, if not a little controversial! I love this drink as it's a really well thought out example of mixology done cleverly. It's essentially a blue margarita, but instead of the salt on the rim we popped it in the baggy. Tequila represents the filming location, the garnish and glass represents the TV show perfectly, it's a fun drink, but most importantly its TASTY!

Original Recipe:

HEISENBERG (LCC MENU)

★ 35ml El Jimador
★ 25ml lime
★ 20ml Velvet Falernum
★ 20ml agave syrup (2:1)

Shake all ingredients and strain into a chemical beaker filled with cubed ice. Garnish with a bag of blue rock salt*.

★ Mix one tablespoon of rock salt with half a teaspoon of blue food colouring and insert into a mini zip baggie.

History:

This LCC-style twist on the legendary Tommy's Margarita was created by JJ Goodman and Joey Medrington back in 2014 when the U.S hit TV series 'Breaking Bad' was making waves all over the world. The blue colour, chemical beaker its served in, and the baggie of blue rock salt which represents the infamous 'Heisenberg' and his blue crystal meth, is enough to get any fan excited! For the full recipe and history on the Tommy's Margarita please check out the Largarita on page 158.

PORN STAR MARTINI

Fizzy, fun and friendly, this bubbly bouncing beverage is a worldwide phenomenon! Vanilla and passion fruit combine perfectly to get your party started right. You've had them at the bar, now it's your turn to make them at home.

INGREDIENTS	
50ml vodka	£1.00
10ml sugar syrup	£0.01
50ml passion fruit juice (Suncrest)	£0.05
50ml apple juice (cloudy)	£0.05
2 drops vanilla extract	£0.04
½ passion fruit pulp	£0.21
25ml prosecco on the side	£0.15
Garnish	£0.15
Total:	**£1.66**

EQUIPMENT:
Scales
Cocktail shaker
Hawthorne strainer
Fine strainer
Spoon

METHOD:
Shake. Add all ingredients to your shaker, add cubed ice, shake and fine strain into a chilled martini glass.

SERVED IN:
Martini glass

ICE:
None

GARNISH:
Half passion fruit

 This baby is by far and away the bestselling cocktail at London Cocktail Clubs, and if you've tried one then you know why! I like to lengthen ours with a touch of apple juice to take away a bit of the classic acidity. Remastering this legendary cocktail for "KITCHEN COCKTAILS" wasn't easy at the start, though this version is by far and away better than almost any you'll try on the high street.

Original Recipe:

PORN STAR MARTINI (LCC MENU)

★ *25ml vodka*
★ *25ml passoa passion fruit liqueur*
★ *20ml cloudy apple juice*
★ *20ml Funkin passion fruit purée*
★ *10ml vanilla syrup*
★ *25ml prosecco*

Add all ingredients (except prosecco) to shaker, shake and fine strain into a chilled martini glass. Half a passion fruit floating to garnish and a 25ml shot glass with prosecco served on the side.

History:

This naughty number gets more action than Ron Jeremy! Created by London bartender Douglas Ankrah in 2002 whilst working at the Maverick Club (the drink was originally called the Maverick Martini). Douglas says he created this drink thinking this is what he imagined a porn star would order. The Champagne is to sip on to balance out the sweetness of the martini itself, though it's often "shot" along with the cocktail itself. This drink is now on every menu from New York to Paris, and even Peckham.

APPLE MARTINI

It's an itsy-bitsy, teeny-weeny, gorgeous green Appletini! If an apple a day truly keeps the doctor away then there's no excuse not to mix up this disco classic! It's back with a vengeance and we are not ashamed of it.

INGREDIENTS	
40ml vodka	£0.80
20ml Apple Sourz	£0.30
40ml apple juice	£0.21
20ml lemon juice	£0.12
15ml runny honey	£0.12
Garnish	£0.05
Total:	£1.60

EQUIPMENT:
Scales
Cocktail shaker
Hawthorne strainer
Fine strainer

METHOD:
Add all ingredients to your shaker, add cubed ice, shake and fine strain into a chilled martini glass.

SERVED IN:
Martini glass

ICE:
None

GARNISH:
6 thinly cut apple slices fanned out and held together with a cocktail pick

Sweet, sour, dry and delicious, a well made Apple Martini is not to be sniffed at. This true taste of the noughties is so simple to make any novice bartender can pick up a shaker and get this one going. The "apple fan" garnish was once revered by top bartenders across the globe, with the goal being thinner the better on your slices. The moisture from the apple should stick the layers together perfectly by themselves, though a classic cocktail pick will give a perfect shape to your "fan" every time you spread out your garnish.

Original Recipe:
SMOKED APPLE MARTINI (LCC)

★ 25ml Bombay Sapphire
★ 15ml Velvet Falernum
★ 15ml apple liqueur
★ 25ml apple juice
★ 15ml sugar syrup
★ 15ml lemon juice
★ ¼ egg white
★ 5-10ml Ardbeg 10yr Scotch whiskey

Shake into a martini glass. Garnish with an apple fan.

History:
A guilty pleasure for most, the Apple Martini, which is commonly referred to as an Appletini, belongs to the "tini" trend of the late 20th century and is nothing like the classic Martini combination of gin and vermouth. Its original name was the Adam's Apple Martini, and was created in 1996 at Lola's West Hollywood restaurant. Try our smoked variation if you're looking to take it up a notch!

COSMOPOLITAN

Carrie Bradshaw and the New York glitterati took this basic martini and made it mainstream! Why not put some sex in your city and shake up a storm that's bound to perk up any pouting prima donna.

INGREDIENTS
40ml Skittles vodka*	£0.90
50ml cranberry juice	£0.05
5ml lime juice	£0.03
5ml sugar syrup	£0.01
Garnish	£0.06
Total:	£1.05

EQUIPMENT:
Scales
Cocktail shaker
Hawthorne strainer
Tea strainer

METHOD:
Add all ingredients to shaker filled with ice, fine strain into chilled coupe glass.

SERVED IN:
Coupe glass

ICE:
None

GARNISH:
Orange twist

★ We don't want you wasting money unnecessarily, so this clever infusion allows you to leave out the triple sec traditionally used in this cocktail. For a rapid infusion put 1 x 55g packet of Skittles into a bottle of vodka (you will need to remove 100ml of vodka to make room for the Skittles) put the cap on and shake for 15 seconds then put through a dishwasher cycle (30 mins), take out and shake again for 15 seconds and you're good to go.

The classic cosmo was in fact very boozy. There was hardly any cranberry in it at all which made it tough to drink, and viewed as very grown up. That almost seems silly now as its reputation has been almost the opposite over the years. For the ultimate finish, try "flaming" your orange peel garnish by simply squeezing the orange zest in front of a lighter, over the glass. It's tricky, but practise makes perfect and once you've mastered it, your guests are guaranteed to be impressed!

Original Recipe:

COSMOPOLITAN (CECCHIN'S RECIPE)

★ 40ml citron vodka
★ 20ml triple sec
★ 20ml lime
★ 20ml cranberry

Add all ingredients to shaker, shake and strain into chilled martini glass. Garnish with lime wedge on the rim.

History:

The honour of creating this modern classic goes to Toby Cecchini who in 1988 put the newly released Absolut Citron to work whilst bartending in Manhattan. However, years later, bartending legend Dale DeGroff perfected his own version of the Cosmo, and with a little help from Carrie Bradshaw and her Sex & The City chums, made the cocktail fashionable. Although DeGroff is often credited with the drink's invention, he has always maintained that he did not create it, but he sure as hell perfected it! Hats off to you Mr DeGroff.

CHARLIE SHEEN

Our favourite bad boy of the big screen loved his margaritas so much we named this one after him. He once said "you either love or you hate, if you live in the middle, you get nothing", well Charlie, we LOVE our margaritas as much as you do, so this ones for you!

INGREDIENTS	
50ml 100% agave tequila	£1.40
30ml lemon juice	£0.18
20ml agave syrup	£0.20
Garnish	£0.55
Total:	£2.33

EQUIPMENT:
Scales
Blender
Spoon

METHOD:
Blend. Add all ingredients to your blender with five ice cubes and blend until smooth.

SERVED IN:
Margarita glass
Shot glass

ICE:
None

GARNISH:
Sea salt rim
Lime wheel
25ml bourbon whiskey

 Blended drinks are remarkably harder to make than people give them credit for. The density is so important if you want the perfect "nipple" on top of your margarita. Too much ice and it will be lumpy and tasteless, too little will leave a watery mess. Make sure your mix moves freely like lava in the blender as you pour it, and if in doubt, add some extra tequila, and always make sure its 100 per cent agave tequila if you don't want to wake up with a sore head!

Original Recipe:

MARGARITA

★ 40ml tequila
★ 20ml Cointreau
★ 20ml lime juice

Shake into a coupe glass with a half salt rim.

History:

The exact origins of the Margarita are unknown, in Spanish it translates as 'daisy', therefore it's believed that the Margarita cocktail is simply a tequila based Daisy. The Daisy dates back to prohibition where cocktails were a necessity in order to make homebrew and moonshine drinkable. A Daisy is typically made with fresh citrus, sweetened with a syrup or liqueur, and strengthened with a base spirit. During prohibition this was usually whatever was on hand.

BRIXTON RIOT

You'll be having a riot after a couple of these fire-starters. This twisted rum punch has been an LCC staple that guarantees to get your guests going. After years of demand it's finally been re-written for you guys to mix merrily (and easily) at home!

INGREDIENTS

25ml white rum	£0.50
25ml golden peach purée*	£0.08
15ml lemon juice	£0.09
25ml lychee juice	£0.03
4 mint leaves	£0.50
25ml cranberry juice	£0.03
15ml sugar syrup	£0.01
Garnish	£0.39
Total:	**£1.63**

★ Golden peach purée: Blend one 410g tin of peaches (including the syrup) with 100ml golden syrup for 30 seconds (You may substitute golden syrup with 100ml of honey or sugar syrup).

Original Recipe:

BRIXTON RIOT (LCC)

- ★ 25ml martin ambrato
- ★ 25ml cranberry
- ★ 15ml lychee liqueur
- ★ 25ml peach purée
- ★ 6 mint leaves
- ★ 10ml wray and nephew

Add all ingredients to a shaker, shake and fine strain into a chilled coupe or martini glass. Garnish with half an emptied passion fruit shell filled with overproof rum (don't forget to set it alight).

EQUIPMENT:
Scales
Cocktail shaker
Hawthorne strainer
Fine strainer
Spoon
Blow torch

METHOD:
Add all ingredients to your shaker, add cubed ice, shake and fine strain into a chilled coupe glass.

SERVED IN:
Coupe glass

ICE:
None

GARNISH:
Emptied out half of passion fruit shell floating in drink, with 10ml overproof rum poured inside and set alight with blow torch

 **JJ SAYS**

I hope it goes without saying that you shouldn't drink this while it's on fire! Flaming cocktails are loads of fun, but be careful what's around you, that you're flaming in a space that is clear, and that your guests know that it's lit when you pass it to them. Feel free to make a wish when you blow it out softly, and upturn the overproof rum, pouring it in to the cocktail for a little extra "heat" the way only "uncle Wray" knows how.

History:

JJ and Andy Mill came up with this drink when opening LCC Goodge Street back in 2010. JJ says: "I was fixated on having a drink with a flaming passion fruit shell floating in a martini glass. I really liked the lychee and peach combo, Andy added vermouth, and hey presto another LCC classic was born."

SHOOTERS

The fastest way to start a party is with shooters, and these oldies are timeless goldies! Whether you're wetting your whistle with work mates, or celebrating a Sunday in the sun with your siblings, try your hand and see where the night takes you.

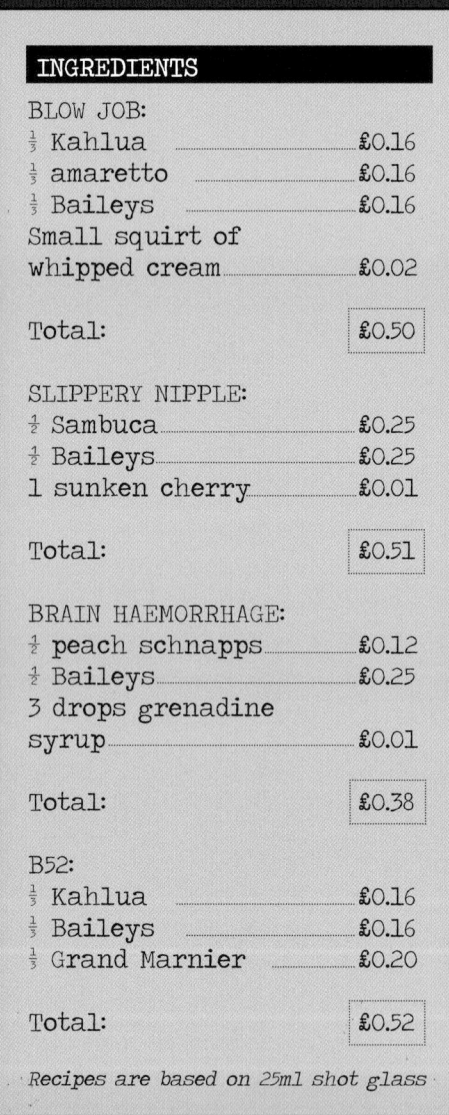

INGREDIENTS

BLOW JOB:
- ⅓ Kahlua — £0.16
- ⅓ amaretto — £0.16
- ⅓ Baileys — £0.16
- Small squirt of whipped cream — £0.02

Total: £0.50

SLIPPERY NIPPLE:
- ½ Sambuca — £0.25
- ½ Baileys — £0.25
- 1 sunken cherry — £0.01

Total: £0.51

BRAIN HAEMORRHAGE:
- ½ peach schnapps — £0.12
- ½ Baileys — £0.25
- 3 drops grenadine syrup — £0.01

Total: £0.38

B52:
- ⅓ Kahlua — £0.16
- ⅓ Baileys — £0.16
- ⅓ Grand Marnier — £0.20

Total: £0.52

Recipes are based on 25ml shot glass

EQUIPMENT:
Spoon

METHOD:
With each shooter, start with the top ingredient then carefully layer remaining ingredients on top of each other using a spoon. With the exception of the brain haemorrhage, where you want to let the grenadine syrup fall through to the bottom creating the effect.

SERVED IN:
Shot glass

ICE:
None

GARNISH:
None

I've always loved shooters, they are a real guilty pleasure. It's important to be aware of how much you're drinking of course, and if you're on a long session, these lower alcohol shooters can steady the pace, but not let you feel like you're missing out. I can't say I ever loved bartending big groups of 20-odd B52s in the middle of service on a Saturday night, though I'd be lying if I said I didn't enjoy one when I'm on the other side of the stick.

History:

A shooter is different from a basic shot of hard liquor, insofar as a shooter is usually mixed with something. According to drinks historian David Wondrich, surprisingly shooters actually emerged pretty recently with the Kamikaze making its appearance in 1976, the B52 in the late 70s and the Slippery Nipple in the 80s. All that's left to say is… shots up!

ZOMBIE APOCALYPSE

Be warned! If you drink two of these you'll turn in to a zombie so proceed with caution! Rum fanatics worldwide have fallen in love with this booze-ridden barbarian of a beverage and I'm sure you will too.

INGREDIENTS	
20ml white rum	£0.40
20ml gold rum	£0.40
20ml dark rum	£0.40
30ml pineapple juice	£0.03
30ml grapefruit juice	£0.03
15ml lime juice	£0.09
2 dashes Angostura bitters	£0.10
20ml grenadine syrup	£0.24
Garnish	£0.05
Total:	**£1.74**

EQUIPMENT:
Scales
Cocktail shaker
Hawthorne strainer
Spoon

METHOD:
Shake and strain.

SERVED IN:
Plastic pumpkin

ICE:
Cubed

GARNISH:
3 gold chocolate coins

JL SAYS

Kia Ora! Tiki drinks, much like tiki bars, hosted by tiki bartenders in their Hawaiian shirts, are a subculture all to themselves. The tiki culture started in Polynesia (Hawaii, New Zealand, Bora Bora, Easter Island, you get the picture, HEAVEN!) and arrived in New Zealand around 1300 AD. "Tiki" is the name given to the first man ever created (as Adam is to Christianity), and the carved mugs we now drink from are in fact the faces of the Maori gods who created him. So put on your loudest shirt, and start sipping!

Original Recipe:

ZOMBIE (DON BEACH RECIPE)

★ 40ml gold Puerto Rican rum
★ 40ml dark Jamaican rum
★ 30ml 151-proof Lemon Hart Demerara rum
★ 20ml lime juice
★ 15ml Falernum
★ 15ml Don's mix (2 parts grapefruit juice to 1 part cinnamon-infused sugar syrup)
★ 1 tsp grenadine
★ 6 drops Pernod
★ Dash of Angostura bitters

Add all ingredients to a blender with a cup of crushed ice, then pour into a tall glass with cubed ice and garnish with a mint sprig.

History:

The Zombie dates back to 1934, when it was invented by Don the Beachcomber at his Hollywood restaurant of the same name. Don supposedly came up with the powerful concoction to serve as liquid CPR for some poor SOB experiencing death by hangover… well, we've all been there. He kept his original recipe a closely guarded secret, to the point of encoding it, not even his staff knew the recipe. Fortunately, at LCC we like to share so we have dug out Don's original recipe for you. You're welcome.

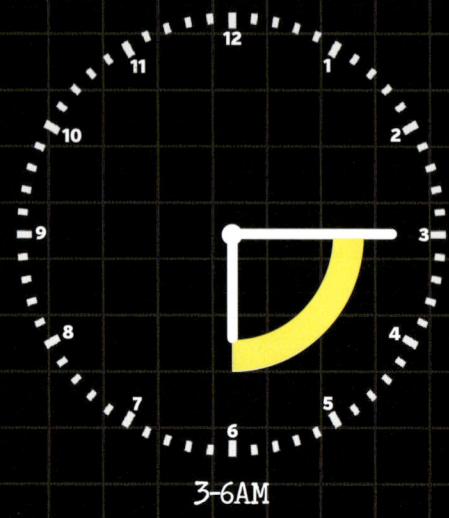

3-6AM

"After the show it's the after party, after the party it's the hotel lobby."

Around about 4, almost all the bloody shops are closed. This chapter is dedicated to get you the greatest drinks out of the dodgiest dimly-lit not-so-convenient stores. Let's be honest, after a long night on the tiles, you don't really want to be shaking your socks off before bed, and these easy corner shop cowboy concoctions will see you through from dusk till dawn.

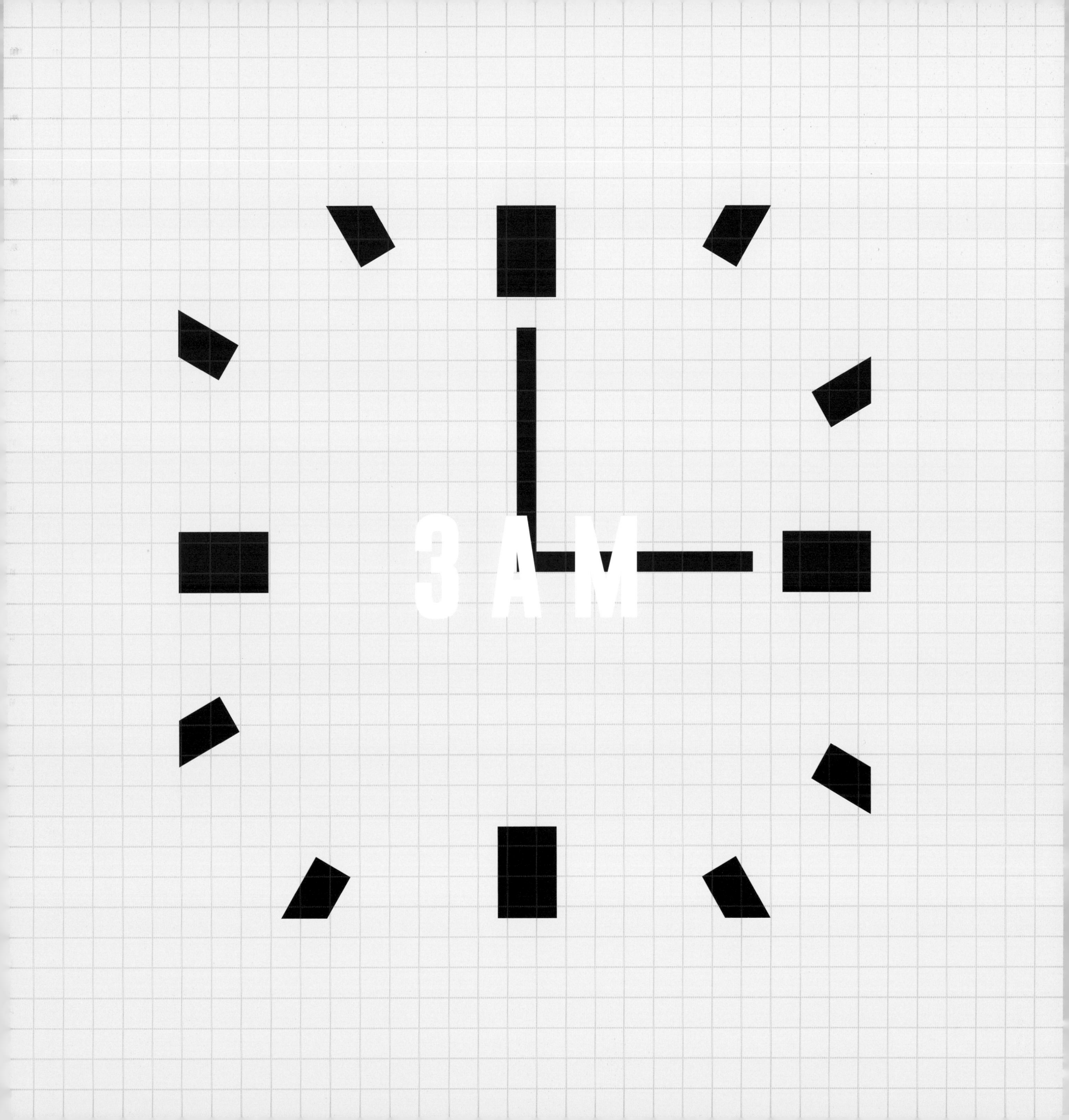

CANDY SHOP COLLINS

Welcome to the candy shop! Where the sweet bursting taste of nostalgia pops through your straws and into your mouths. You can literally mix up any candy to make this, but if like me you're a Haribo nerd, then chuck in some Starmix and get mixing.

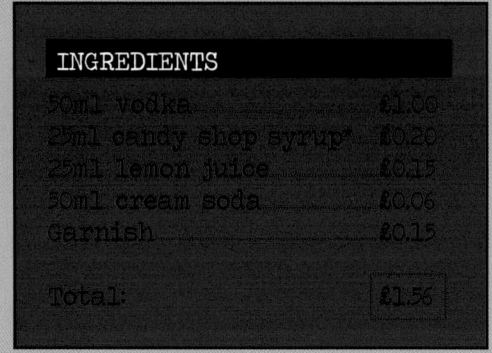

INGREDIENTS	
50ml vodka	£1.00
25ml candy shop syrup*	£0.20
25ml lemon juice	£0.15
50ml cream soda	£0.06
Garnish	£0.15
Total:	£1.56

★ Candy shop syrup: In a saucepan add 25g of Haribo for every 100ml of sugar syrup. Simmer until the sweets have dissolved, let it cool, place in a bottle or kilner jar and store in the fridge (lasts up to 6 weeks).

EQUIPMENT:
Scales
Spoon

METHOD:
Add first three ingredients to Collins glass filled with ice, stir, then top with cream soda.

SERVED IN:
Collins glass

ICE:
Cubed

GARNISH:
1 Drumstick lolly
1 Sherbet flying saucer
3 Love Hearts
...but really, anything goes!

 So, this is simply mixology 101. Change the spirit or change the soda it's up to you, but I love playing with sugars. Add any sweets that you love to the same amount of water and boil. The result is a syrup that will make me grin from ear to ear, especially when mixed with your favourite spirit!

Original Recipe:

MOSCOW MULE

★ 50ml vodka
★ 15ml lime
★ 150ml fiery ginger beer

Pour the vodka and lime into a copper mug, fill with cubed ice and top with ginger beer. Garnish with a lime wedge.

History:

The most popular story in circulation is of John G. Martin who, in 1939, had acquired the rights to Smirnoff vodka via a small Connecticut based liquor and food distributor. At the same time a good friend of his, Jack Morgan, who owned Hollywood's famous British pub, the Cock'n'Bull Salon on Sunset Strip, was trying to launch his own brand of ginger beer but sales were not going well. They met up, had a 'eureka' moment, and the rest as they say is history.

STONE FRUIT SOUR

Roald Dahl would be proud of this one! Some of my favourite flavours harmoniously balanced in the same glass. I love apricot and think it's one of the most underused flavours in gastronomy as a whole. Not to worry, it's here to stay in this rich, mouth-watering cocktail that will bring you back for more!

INGREDIENTS

50ml gin	£1.00
2 tsp apricot jam	£0.10
15ml runny honey	£0.12
20ml lemon juice	£0.12
50ml tinned peach purée*	£0.13
1 egg white	£0.15
Garnish	£0.01
Total:	£1.63

EQUIPMENT:
Scales
Spoon
Cocktail shaker
Hawthorne strainer
Fine strainer

METHOD:
Add all ingredients to shaker filled with ice, fine strain into rocks glass filled with cubed ice.

SERVED IN:
Rocks glass

ICE:
Cubed

GARNISH:
Large mint leaf

★ Tinned peach purée: Blend one 410g tin of tinned peaches (including syrup) for 30 seconds, pour into an empty bottle or kilner jar and store in the fridge (lasts up to 2 weeks).

 This was one of my first original drinks way back in 2006 while working at Teatro in Soho. Mixologists spend a long time tinkering with cocktails, swapping between ingredients, measurements and flavours. It's very rare you're completely blown away by a cocktail on its first run, but the stone fruit sour did just that.

Original Recipe:

GIN RICKEY

★ *50ml bourbon*
★ *½ lime*
★ *soda*

Add the bourbon, squeeze the lime in and drop the shell in, add cubed ice and stir, then top with soda.

History:

Often referred to simply as "a rickey", the Gin Rickey was famously concocted at Shoomaker's bar in Washington D.C. in the 1880s by bartender George A. Williamson. It was there that Missouri-born lobbyist Colonel Joe Rickey took to a mix of rye whiskey, fizzy water and lemon juice on the rocks. As the story goes, in 1883 Missouri Rep. William Henry Hatch ordered "that Joe Rickey drink" with half a lime replacing the lemon juice. This new variation caught on as did gin in replacement of bourbon.

HONEY BEE
FIZZ

A light and refreshing silver gin fizz with the subtle sweetness of honey. This is guaranteed to get the party buzzzzzzzzing (sorry, not sorry). It's easy to make, but more importantly, easy to impress, I love this drink!

INGREDIENTS

50ml gin	£1.00
20ml lemon juice	£0.12
20ml runny honey	£0.16
1 egg white	£0.15
50ml soda water	£0.05
Garnish	£0.05
Total:	£1.53

EQUIPMENT:
Scales
Spoon
Cocktail shaker
Hawthorne strainer

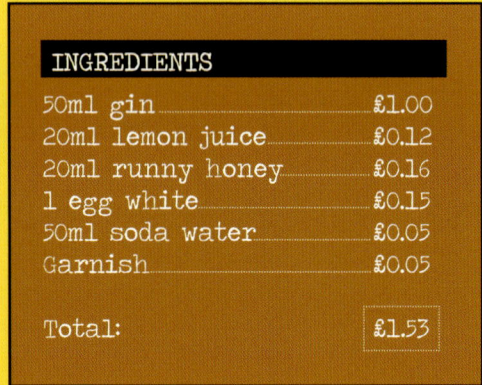

METHOD:
Shake all the ingredients (except the soda). Strain into a chilled champagne flute and top with soda water.

SERVED IN:
Flute glass

ICE:
None

GARNISH:
Lemon zest

 My obsession with honey has no boundaries! This naturally-occurring nectar that's harvested by billions of bees from the beautiful flowers that sprawl across the world simply blows my mind. Its variations are massive, so select your honey carefully. Acacia honey from the supermarket will do a great job, but find one locally by an organic grower and your life will change forever. I literally have it in everything!

Original Recipe:
BEE'S KNEES

★ 50ml gin
★ 20ml lemon juice
★ 15ml honey syrup

Shake into a martini glass and garnish with a lemon twist.

History:

The origin of the Bee's Knees cocktail is unfortunately lost to history. Did nobody write anything down back in the day? What we do know is that it popped up sometime during Prohibition, and the name comes from prohibition slang meaning 'the best'. Like many cocktails from that era, it was invented as a way of hiding the scent and flavour of poor quality homemade spirits, in this case bathtub gin. It's one of the first recorded cocktails to make use of honey. Interesting fact, honey is the only food source produced by an insect that is consumed by humans.

MINTLESS MOJITO

The Mojito is THE most recognisable and popular cocktail on the planet and this recipe is killer! When you can't find fresh mint at the 24-hour convenience shop, don't panic we've got your back!

INGREDIENTS	
50ml white rum	£1.00
30ml Polo Mint syrup*	£0.05
6 lime wedges	£0.18
50ml soda	£0.05
Garnish	£0.04
Total:	£1.32

★ Polo Mint syrup: In a saucepan add 1 x 34g pack of Polo Mints for every 100ml of sugar syrup (you may also use Sugar Free Polo Mints to make this syrup). Simmer until the mints have dissolved, let it cool, place in a bottle or kilner jar and store in the fridge (lasts up to 6 weeks).

EQUIPMENT:
Scales
Spoon
Muddler

METHOD:
Muddle lime wedges in bottom of Collins glass, add Polo Mint syrup and rum, fill with cubed ice, stir, then top with soda.

SERVED IN:
Collins glass

ICE:
Cubed

GARNISH:
3 Polo Mints
Mint sprig (if you can find it at 3am)

 **SAYS**
I've made and sold more mojitos than I care to imagine, and that's of course because this drink is incredible and I appreciate why the world is so obsessed with it! Trying to mix it with cubed ice for a change blew my mind, but I'm really happy with the results! If Polos aren't your bag, I strongly recommend Trebor (no pun intended).

Original Recipe:

MOJITO (LCC)

★ 50ml white rum
★ 25ml sugar syrup
★ 6 lime wedges (½)
★ 12 mint leaves
★ 3 dashes Angostura bitters

Muddle lime wedges in the bottom of a Collins glass, add mint leaves (slap to release aroma), add sugar and rum, fill two-thirds with crushed ice, churn with spoon, cap with crushed ice and garnish with a mint sprig and float Angostura bitters on top.

History:

This drink dates back to the time of the Spanish Armada in the late 1500s. Its origins stem from an early version of the Mojito called El Draque (the dragon), named after Sir Francis Drake who enjoyed the concoction while causing havoc against the Spanish fleets. It was made from firewater (aguardiente, a crude form of rum) sugar, lime and mint. It became known as the Mojito in Cuba in the 1800s, probably inspired by the lime-infused Cuban seasoning called Mojo, and popularised by Don Facundo Bacardi when his now famous rum replaced the firewater around the late 1800s.

TOM COLLINS

The Tom Collins is a go-to for every great bartender. When you're not sure what to order, this light, refreshing, and simply stunning drink will start your night off perfectly, or even end it!

INGREDIENTS

50ml gin	£1.00
25ml lemon juice	£0.15
20ml sugar syrup*	£0.02
50ml soda water	£0.05
Garnish	£0.04
Total:	**£1.26**

* In a saucepan add 500ml caster sugar to 500ml of hot water from the kettle, gently simmer until all the sugar has dissolved and the syrup is clear. Let it cool, then pour into an empty bottle and refrigerate (lasts up to 6 weeks).

EQUIPMENT:
Scales
Spoon

METHOD:
Add first three ingredients to Collins glass filled with ice, stir, then top with soda.

SERVED IN:
Collins glass

ICE:
Cubed

GARNISH:
Lemon wheel

JC SAYS

Tom Collins is the gold standard of a cocktail and, in fact, a bartender. Though a simple drink to get right, you can taste a true mixologist through this cocktail when they balance the four elements of spirit, sweet, sour and dilution harmoniously. When I drop into a new bar, or in fact, meet a bartender for the first time, this is the drink I almost always order. Top bartenders love the challenge and never fail me.

Original Recipe:

JOHN COLLINS

★ 50ml Dutch gin
★ 20ml lemon
★ 20ml sugar syrup
★ 50ml top with soda

Add first three ingredients into a shaker, shake and strain into a tall glass filled with cubed ice. Top with soda water and garnish with a lemon wheel.

History:

The Tom Collins first appeared on paper in Jerry Thomas's 1876 version of the 'Bon Vivant's Companion', stating few drinks are as refreshing on a summer afternoon. And the name? A certain John Collins, who was a waiter at Limmer's Old House in London, got his name hitched to this historic drink originally made with Dutch gin. However, his name got lost along the way when Old Tom gin became the norm for mixing this drink, poor guy… well at least we gave him a mention.

LAGERITA

A bartender favourite, this is exactly what is says on the tin! A base mix of a Tommy's Margarita topped up with ice cold beer! Don't underestimate it. This cocktail is designed for that "aaaaaaaaarrrrrgggggghhhh" moment.

INGREDIENTS

50ml 100% agave tequila	£1.40
25ml lime juice	£0.15
15ml agave syrup	£0.15
150ml lager	£0.60
Garnish	£0.05
Total:	£2.35

EQUIPMENT:
Scales
Spoon
Cocktail shaker
Hawthorne strainer

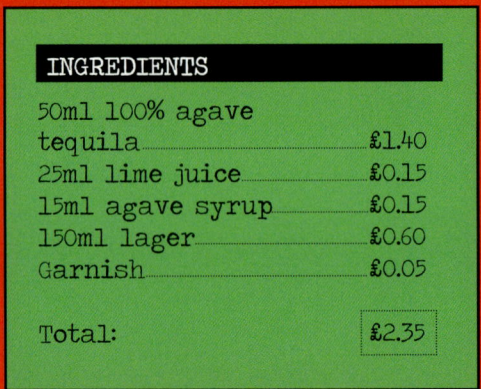

METHOD:
Shake first three ingredeints, strain into half pint glass filled with cubed ice, then top up with lager.

SERVED IN:
Half pint glass

ICE:
Cubed

GARNISH:
Lime wheel
Mexican sombrero (wearing it is optional)

 I was first served this cocktail by Gregor de Gruyther back in 2004 at Sohos LAB bar, which was debatably the most influential bar in living history, packed with the most influential bartenders in living history to boot! Not only will I never forget this drink, but I'll never forget how it was served. It's amazing the imprint a great bartender can have in your life.

Original Recipe:

TOMMY'S MARGARITA

★ 60ml Tequila (Reposado)
★ 30ml lime juice
★ 15ml agave syrup

Shake all ingredients and strain into a rocks glass with cubed ice. Garnish with a lime wedge.

History:

UK bartender Ben Reed is credited with the invention of this concoction in 2001. He reckons a dark Mexican beer is the best tipple for topping off a classic Margarita. Be warned though, as Reed delicately puts it: "You're off your head after one of them!" The Tommy's Margarita itself was created in the early 1990s by Julio Bermejo at Tommy's bar in San Fransisco. Julio subs out the triple sec in the classic Margarita for agave syrup (the honey like sweetener that naturally comes from the agave plant that makes tequila) and serves the drink short over ice.

DARK & STORMY

A basic drink if ever there was one! So why are some so great and others so average? The right rum must have the right ginger beer, the right ginger beer must have the right lime. You'll never have a bad one which is the good news, but can you mix the best?

INGREDIENTS

50ml premium rum	£1.50
150ml ginger beer	£0.50
3 dashes Angostura bitters	£0.15
2 squeezed lime wedges	£0.06
Garnish	£0.03
Total:	£2.24

EQUIPMENT:
Scales
Spoon

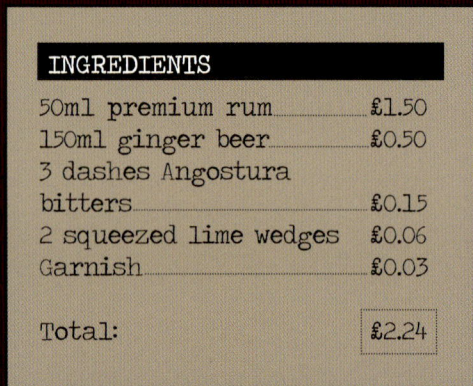

METHOD:
Squeeze the juice of two lime wedges into a Collins glass filled with cubed ice, then pour the ginger beer. Finally layer with dark rum and Angostura bitters.

SERVED IN:
Collins glass

ICE:
Cubed

GARNISH:
1 lime wedge

 I always pick my favourite drink by the time of day, the climate, or the country that I'm in, but very few drinks can appease all of the above for me, and this is certainly one of them. I personally love it with fiery ginger beer, dark rum, and loads of lime and Angostura bitters. As the ice melts this drink seems to get better by the sip.

Original Recipe:

DARK 'N' STORMY

★ *50ml Goslings Black Seal Rum*
★ *150ml Ginger Beer*

Pour rum into a tall glass filled with cubed ice, and then top up with ginger beer. Garnish with a lime wedge.

History:

The Gosling Brothers Ltd of Bermuda, have registered the trademark in the U.S since 1991 for the cocktail name Dark 'N' Stormy, though the drink has certainly been around much longer with records of ginger beer production dating back to the mid 1700s in England's very own Yorkshire. The British navy would later take the recipes to the Americas in the 19th century where rum was added with lime in the Caribbean. The drink apparently got its name from an old sailor who compared the drink to a storm cloud, the rum (the dark) and the ginger beer (the stormy).

ICED TEAS

Iced teas are super-easy to make and really hit the spot when you have a serious thirst. They were the "it" drinks category during the disco era, as the ideal drink to light a fire on the dancefloor. After hours throw some booze in, and some lemon, and top with soda. These usual suspects should give you some inspiration how to pull off any iced tea.

INGREDIENTS

LONG ISLAND ICED TEA
10ml vodka	£0.21
10ml gin	£0.21
10ml rum	£0.21
10ml Triple Sec	£0.18
10ml tequila	£0.21
20ml lemon juice	£0.14
20ml sugar syrup**	£0.04
75ml Diet Coke	£0.07
Lemon wheel garnish	£0.04
Total:	**£1.31**

BEVERLY HILLS ICED TEA
20ml gin	£0.42
20ml vodka	£0.42
30ml Triple Sec	£0.18
20ml lime juice	£0.20
20ml sugar syrup**	£0.04
50ml Champagne	£1.30
Lime wedge garnish	£0.04
Total:	**£2.60**

LONG BEACH ICED TEA
10ml vodka	£0.21
10ml gin	£0.21
10ml rum	£0.21
10ml tequila	£0.21
10ml Triple Sec	£0.18
15ml lemon juice	£0.14
50ml cranberry juice	£0.04
Lime wedge garnish	£0.04
Total:	**£1.24**

TOKYO ICED TEA
10ml vodka	£0.21
10ml gin	£0.21
10ml rum	£0.21
10ml Triple Sec	£0.18
10ml tequila	£0.21
10ml Midori	£0.19
20ml lime juice	£0.20
75ml lemonade	£0.02
Mint leaf garnish	£0.01
Total:	**£1.44**

★ For all four of these iced teas, pour every ingredient (expect the last one) over cubed ice in a tall glass. Stir six times and then gently pour the last ingredient on top (e.g. lemonade for the Tokyo Iced Tea).

★★ In a saucepan add 500ml caster sugar to 500ml of hot water from the kettle, gently simmer until all the sugar has dissolved and the syrup is clear. Let it cool, then pour into an empty bottle and refrigerate (lasts up to 6 weeks).

EQUIPMENT:
Scales
Spoon
Cocktail shaker
Hawthorne strainer

METHOD:
Build.

SERVED IN:
Collins glass

ICE:
Cubed

LCC SAYS

I insisted on putting the Long Island Iced Tea back on the LCC menus despite some rolling eyes. The truth is the "lads" love them. It's so important to me that when anyone picks up an LCC menu that they feel at ease, and the LIIT does that for so many likely lads desperately trying to impress their first date. It's one of our top sellers to date!

History:

Robert "Rosebud" Butt claims to have invented The Long Island Iced Tea in a competition entry in 1972, whilst he was working at the Oak Beach Inn on New York's Long Island. The competition challenged bartenders to make a drink with triple sec, which doesn't sound that hard to us, but hey, he won, and the Long Island Iced Tea is served in bars all over the globe.

6-9AM

"Growing up as a bartender, I've seen, heard and tasted it all before when it comes to hangover cures. From the sublime to the simply savage, the following few solutions should bounce you back, so there's no need to call an ambulance. Crawl out from under the duvet, open the curtains and slide yourself into the kitchen to knock up a round of these for you and your mates… Not all heroes wear capes!"

HOUSE BLOODY MARY

We can't start the Hangover Cures chapter without the classic Bloody Mary. This cocktail has been getting people out of bed since the 1920s. Make a big jug of this one and add as much spice as you can handle!

INGREDIENTS

25ml vodka	£0.50
125ml tomato juice	£0.12
10 dashes Worcester sauce	£0.20
3 dashes Tabasco	£0.15
Pinch celery salt	£0.01
Pinch black pepper	£0.01
5ml lemon juice	£0.03
Garnish	£0.12
Total:	**£1.14**

EQUIPMENT:
Scales
Glass jug
Wooden spoon

METHOD:
Stir. Add all ingredients to glass jug, fill with cubed ice, stir thoroughly with a wooden spoon and pour into rocks glass filled with cubed ice. You can multiply the recipe depending on how many people you are serving.

SERVED IN:
Rocks glass

ICE:
Cubed

GARNISH:
Celery stick
Lemon wedge
Cucumber slice
½ baby vine tomato
Pinch of pepper

 **JJ SAYS** — I went to school in Worcester from the age of 12; it's where I also mixed my first cocktail at Keystons Café aged just 17. Worcester is the home of the Morgan car, the Warriors rugby team and of course, the world famous sauce! There's a reason I put a lot in, and it's not just because I'm biased (not 100 per cent anyway), it's because of the incredible, rich depth of flavour that you'd be a fool to mix without.

Original Recipe:

BLOODY MARY

★ 50ml vodka
★ 100ml tomato juice
★ 20ml lemon juice
★ 3 dashes tabasco
★ 3 dashes Worcestershire sauce
★ pinch black pepper
★ pinch salt

Build in a highball glass with cubed ice. Garnish with celery, a cherry tomato and pepper.

History:

The young fellow most often associated with the drink's creation is Fernand Petiot whilst bartending at Harry's New York Bar in Paris during the 1920s. Although cocktail historians argue he simply spiced up an existing and well-established combo of vodka and tomato juice. As for the name, the drink was often referred to as a 'bucket of blood' or 'mary rose', and its believed the final name came from a combination of the two. Conveniently 1st January is National Bloody Mary Day, which is observed around the globe. Be sure to jot that one in your diary!

ALL-DAY BREAKFAST
BLOODY MARY

There's only a few things that get me out of bed on a Saturday these days, a great Bloody Mary is one and an all-day breakfast is another! HP sauce uses Worcester in its blend, plus a splash of tomato. This slightly sweet mary goes down better than it might read to some!

INGREDIENTS	
25ml vodka	£0.50
125ml tomato juice	£0.12
25ml HP Sauce	£0.10
3 dashes Tabasco	£0.15
Pinch sea salt	£0.01
Pinch black pepper	£0.01
10ml tomato ketchup	£0.03
Garnish	£0.17
Total:	£1.09

EQUIPMENT:
Scales
Spoon
Glass jug
Wooden spoon

METHOD:
Stir. Add all ingredients to glass jug, fill with cubed ice, stir thoroughly with a wooden spoon and pour into baked beans tin filled with cubed ice. You can multiply the recipe depending on how many people you are serving.

SERVED IN:
Baked beans tin

ICE:
Cubed

GARNISH:
Slice of crisp streaky bacon
Grilled tomato
Lemon slice

Original Recipe:

JJ'S ULTIMATE ALL-DAY FULL ENGLISH

★ 1 Cumberland sausage
★ 4 rashers Smoked streaky bacon
★ 2 black pudding   ★ 2 hash browns
★ 1 fried egg   ★ 1 grilled tomato
★ 1 slice fried bread (cut into 4 triangles)
★ 2 large Mushrooms (chopped and seared)
★ ½ can of baked beans

The key to making an awesome full English is timing, everything needs to be ready at the same time. The sausages take the longest so they need cooking first along with the streaky bacon. My grandmother's trick with fried bread (which should be cooked last to mop up all the flavour from the pan) was to fry one side so its nice and crispy and keep the other side soft. Try it you wont regret it.

 **JJ SAYS**
I live in Camden directly above a "greasy spoon" and the smell is wonderfully intoxicating to me. It's not unusual to see me in my pyjamas and flip-flops brandishing one of my own plates tip-toeing in to get it piled high so I can return to the man cave I've built on the sofa moments earlier. I really love this drink; if the Worcestershire sauce bottle's empty I reach straight for my HP, before lathering my sausages with the same oozing liquid.

History:

The phrase 'full English breakfast', or 'Full Monty', often specifically denotes a breakfast including everything on offer. The latter name became popular after World War II, when British Army general Bernard Montgomery (nicknamed Monty) was said to have started every day with a full English breakfast when in battle.

SUNDAY ROAST
BLOODY MARY

Sundays roast and a Bloody Mary is as English as tea and crumpets, if not more so. So why not add a little beef stock to our favourite hangover cure? Red wine and horseradish work wonders while mustard is certainly the connoisseurs' choice of spice on a Sunday!

INGREDIENTS

25ml bourbon	£0.50
15ml lemon	£0.09
4 dashes Worcestershire sauce	£0.08
2 tsp horseradish	£0.04
1 tsp mustard	£0.02
Pinch black pepper	£0.01
Pinch sea salt	£0.01
10ml red wine	£0.05
100ml tomato juice	£0.10
2 tsp beef stock cube	£0.20
1 sprig of rosemary	£0.10
Garnish	£0.12
Total:	£1.32

EQUIPMENT:
Scales
Wooden spoon
Glass jug
Mixing glass

METHOD:
Stir. Add all ingredients to glass jug, fill with cubed ice, stir thoroughly with a wooden spoon and pour into rocks glass filled with cubed ice. You can multiply the recipe depending on how many people you are serving.

SERVED IN:
Rocks glass

ICE:
Cubed

GARNISH:
Aunt Bessie's Yorkshire pudding

 I created this drink for the guys at Eurostar and it went down a storm! We named it "les rosbif", a cheeky nod to our friendly "frogs" across the pond. The one day a week most families growing up insist on sharing is a Sunday, and whether you're playing football in the garden or reading a paper in the lounge, we all come running to the call of "lunch is ready" to tuck in to our meat and two veg with all the trimmings.

Original Recipe:
BULL SHOT
- 60ml vodka
- 100ml chilled beef bouillion
- Dash of lemon
- 3 dashes Worcester sauce
- 3 dashes Tabasco
- Pinch of ground black pepper

Add all ingredients to a shaker, add ice, shake and strain into a highball filled with cubed ice. Garnish with a lemon wedge and pinch of ground black pepper.

History:

If you take the tomato juice out of a Bloody Mary and replace it with beef broth you have yourself a bull shot. It's believed to have been created around 1952 at Detroit's Caucus Club and by the late 1950s it had exploded onto the scene thanks to its popularity in Hollywood. The 1971 film Clockwork Orange features the drink and helped it remain popular until the early 1980s.

THE CURRY MARY

A great curry is never about the heat, it's always about the spice, just like a great Bloody Mary! Where would we be as a nation without our favourite Saturday night takeaway? Don't bin the leftovers along with the mini salad bag. Pop a couple of heaped spoons into your Bloody Mary the next day to add a depth of flavour you'll crave all week.

INGREDIENTS

25ml gin	£0.50
125ml tomato juice	£0.12
Pinch coriander powder	£0.01
2 pinches cayenne pepper powder	£0.02
Pinch cumin powder	£0.01
Pinch sea salt	£0.01
20ml lime juice	£0.12
20ml coconut milk	£0.04
2 tsp bhuna sauce	£0.02
Garnish	£0.22
Total:	£1.07

EQUIPMENT:
Scales
Wooden spoon
Glass jug

METHOD:
Stir. Add all ingredients to glass jug, fill with cubed ice, stir thoroughly with a wooden spoon and pour into vintage mug filled with cubed ice. You can multiply the recipe depending on how many people you are serving.

SERVED IN:
Vintage Indian coffee mug

ICE:
Cubed

GARNISH:
Lime wedge
Tomato slice
Coriander sprig
¼ vegetable samosa

Being born in Birmingham, my fondest Saturdays were in a curry house with my dad after a day at Villa Park watching my beloved football team; it would either make my week or break my heart. "Birmingham has better curry than India" my dad proudly believes. With the unbelievable curries you can get in the Midlands, there's no reason to question him!

Original Recipe:

CAESAR

- 50m vodka
- 150ml clamato juice
- 8 drops hot pepper sauce (cayenne based)
- 4 dashes Worcester sauce
- 2 pinches of celery salt
- 1 pinch of ground black pepper

Add all ingredients to a shaker, add ice, shake and strain into a tall glass filled with cubed ice. Garnish with a celery stick and lime wedge.

History:

Although very similar to a Bloody Mary, the Caesar has a very unique flavour, which comes from a combination of hot sauce and clamato juice. It was invented in 1969 by Walter Chell of the Calgary Inn (known today as the Westin Hotel) in Calgary, Alberta, Canada. The hotel had just opened a new Italian restaurant for which Chell was tasked with creating a new signature drink. Chell was inspired by the flavours of spaghetti vongole (spaghetti and clams), and named the drink after the Roman Emperor Julius Caesar.

RED-EYE

This rite of passage is a bartender favourite...ish. A whole egg thrown neatly in a mix of spiced tomato and beer is not for the faint-hearted. It starts well, but finishes rough, so unleash your inner Rocky Balboa and see it through to the end.

INGREDIENTS	
300ml lager	£1.25
150ml tomato juice	£0.15
4 dashes Worcestershire sauce	£0.08
3 dashes Tabasco	£0.15
1 whole egg	0.15
Total:	£1.78

EQUIPMENT:
Scales
Spoon

METHOD:
Build. Add first 4 ingredients to pint glass, and gently mix together (its important that the beer is cold), then crack the whole egg in last.

SERVED IN:
Pint glass

ICE:
None

GARNISH:
None

 **SAYS** I've drank more of these than I need to, but a blend of peer pressure and camaraderie will find you in front of a few Red-eyes while working as a professional cocktail bartender. To gain maximum benefit from this, it's all about the technique. Drink the first three-quarters, then take on the egg last! Don't choke, or you'll be the laughing stock of the room.

Original Recipe:

MICHELADA (TRADITIONAL RECIPE)

★ 1 bottle Mexican lager (Modelo is typical)
★ 100ml clamato juice
★ Juice of 1 lime
★ 4 dashes Worcestershire sauce
★ ¼ tsp Maggi sauce (or soy sauce)
★ 2-4 dashes Mexican hot sauce
★ 1 tsp Tajin seasoning (or salt)

Pour the Tajin on a small plate, rub a lime wedge around the rim of a beer mug, then press the rim into the Tajin to coat it. Build remaining ingredients (except beer) in the glass, add cubed ice, then top with beer. Garnish with a slice of lime.

History:

The Michelada originated in Mexico in the 1960s and was (back then) a heavy salty drink to give you exactly what you need when you're feeling a little rough from the night before. The 1988 film Cocktail starring Tom Cruise as cocky bartender Brian Flanagan has its own take on the Michelada called a Red Eye, which adds a whole egg into the equation. Many drinks use the name, but it's very likely that Cocktail launched this variation into the world. As Flanagan's witty mentor Doug Coughlin says in the film, "beer is for breakfast around here, drink or be gone!"

BREAKFAST MIMOSA

Take two amazing breakfast cocktails, put them together and what do you get? Taking the best bits from the Breakfast Martini and the fizzy bits from the Mimosa, what's not to love? Morning everyone…!

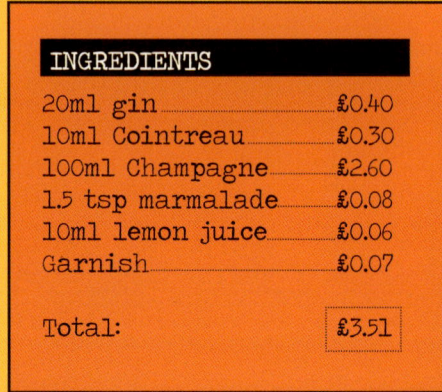

INGREDIENTS	
20ml gin	£0.40
10ml Cointreau	£0.30
100ml Champagne	£2.60
1.5 tsp marmalade	£0.08
10ml lemon juice	£0.06
Garnish	£0.07
Total:	£3.51

EQUIPMENT:
Scales
Spoon
Cocktail Shaker
Hawthorne Strainer

METHOD:
Shake. Add all ingredients to your shaker, add cubed ice, shake and strain into a chilled wine goblet.

SERVED IN:
Large wine goblet

ICE:
Cubed

GARNISH:
Orange wheel
Marmalade on triangle toast

 **SAYS**

Salvatore is a bartender I've always looked up to and can now call a mate. Where the simple Mimosa fell short, adding a thick cut rich marmalade did all the rest. Calabrese's mix is already perfect so I didn't have to do much else, though I love the length, and the Champagne somehow makes me feel less guilty about drinking a couple over brunch.

Original Recipes:

MIMOSA
- 60ml orange juice
- 60ml prosecco

Combine and serve into a flute glass.

BREAKFAST MARTINI
- 30ml gin
- 20ml Cointreau
- 20ml lemon juice
- 1.5 tsp marmalade

Shake and serve in a coupe glass with an orange twist for garnish.

History:

The Breakfast Martini is without doubt the most famous marmalade cocktail. It was created by celebrity bartender Salvatore Calabrese in 1996 at the Library Bar in London. He invented this gin-based drink thanks to his wife Susan's observation that breakfast was not complete without British marmalade. The Mimosa was believed to have been invented circa 1925 in the Hôtel Ritz, Paris by Frank Meier. Although we don't know who came up with the name, we do know that the drink was named after a pretty Australian yellow-orange shrub known as Acacia dealbata, which is nicknamed… you guessed it, Mimosa.

THE BARTENDER'S
BREAKFAST

Who better to ask the best way to cure a hangover than a bartender. Years in the game takes its toll, but all bartenders have to put their game faces on regardless. So this…well… completely irresponsible little number will put you right back on your feet, and in some cases, bring you back from the dead.

INGREDIENTS

50ml 100% agave tequila	£1.40
100ml Irn Bru	£0.10
2 Vitamin C & Zinc	£0.20
1 Berocca	£0.30
100ml orange juice	£0.10
20ml lime juice	£0.12
Total:	£2.22

EQUIPMENT:
Scales

METHOD:
Build. Throw all the ingredients into a glass (make sure the Irn Bru and orange juice are chilled) and wait until the sound of hissing bubbles stops, then down it.

SERVED IN:
Measuring beaker

ICE:
None

GARNISH:
3 warm hugs
1 bacon sandwich
2 ibuprofen
1 double shot of espresso
Any hopes and dreams

The ingredients say it all… Get one of these down you if you're on an AFD.! (All F*****g Day). Created specifically for this book. We asked the bartending community what is the first drink they make for themselves to get them back in the game after a big Friday shift and ready for an even bigger Saturday! The answers came in their droves and I've mixed all these ideas together and come up with the perfect combination to bring you back to life.

History:

Can an alcoholic drink cure a hangover? Well the expression 'hair of the dog' (shortening of 'a hair of the dog that bit you') would certainly have you believe so. It comes from an old belief that someone bitten by a rabid dog could be cured of rabies by taking an elixir containing some of the dog's hair. The theory is, although alcohol may be to blame for the hangover (as the dog is for the attack), a smaller portion of the same will act as a cure. We should mention there is no scientific evidence that this cure works. But what the heck does 'science' know right?!

BACON & EGG MARTINI

We all love a whiskey sour, so why not try this legendary London Cocktail Club twist?! The smoky taste of bacon is paired with the sweetness of maple syrup and lengthened with egg whites. In the USA this is breakfast without the panckakes!

INGREDIENTS

50ml Jack Daniels washed with bacon*	£1.14
20ml maple syrup	£0.20
20ml lemon juice	£0.12
1 dash orange bitters	£0.05
1 egg white	£0.15
Garnish	£0.12
Total:	**£1.78**

★ 30ml of fresh bacon fat - smoked streaky is best (keep the crispy bacon for garnish) - per 700ml bottle of Jack Daniels. Combine the fat and bourbon in a large non-reactive container and shake vigorously. Let it sit for 4 hours, then place in the freezer for 4 hours. Remove solid fat from the top and fine strain through a cheesecloth or coffee filter and re-bottle.

EQUIPMENT:
Scales
Cocktail shaker
Hawthorne strainer

METHOD:
Shake. Add all ingredients to your shaker, add cubed ice, shake and strain into a chilled coupe glass.

SERVED IN:
Coupe glass

ICE:
None

GARNISH:
Slice of crispy streaky bacon
Haribo egg

I won't lie to you, when I wrote this drink it was a bit of a laugh, it tasted great, but it was in response to a then new technique of "fat washing". Essentially heating fatty stuff like popcorn up so that it became thinner, allowing it to infuse with alcohol. Bourbon made the most sense to infuse bacon; maple syrup made the most sense to sweeten bourbon, and before we knew it, the phone wouldn't stop ringing for media requests.

Original Recipe:

WHISKEY SOUR (JERRY THOMAS 1862)

★ 1 heaped tsp of powdered white sugar
★ Juice of half a small lemon
★ 1 wine glass of Bourbon or rye whiskey

Fill the glass full of shaved ice, shake up and strain into a claret glass. Ornament with berries.

History:

Although the Whiskey Sour appears in the 1862 book 'The Bon Vivants Guide' by Jerry Thomas, it's believed to have been around for many years prior. Many drinks historians believe it to be a relative of the navy grog (rum, lime and sugar) introduced in 1740 by Admiral Edward Vernon to combat scurvy. When sailors returned back to England, gin was added in place of rum and in America it was whiskey. These days its common practice to add egg white, which makes it a Boston Sour, and if you go one extra and float red wine on top of the eggy foam you have yourself a New York Sour.

9AM-12PM

"We all know the pitfalls of over-indulgence so it only felt fitting that I gave you some great drinks to fix up and look sharp. Once you take the booze out of a cocktail you can find lots of great flavours that are full of vitamins and nutrients to cleanse your soul and get the devil off your shoulder. Whether you're a protein-pounding fitness freak or a juice-diet disciple, I've provided the recipe that will put the power back into your punch and reawaken your weekend warrior."

VICTORIA'S SECRET

Here's one for the kale slurping, celery munching, side salad loving, juice freaks; God knows I wish I could be one! But never fear, I've harnessed all the goodness, but delivered on all the taste for this light, and refreshing smoothie that will help get your beach body ready for your next Ibiza blowout!

INGREDIENTS

½ avocado	£0.40
25g celery	£0.06
50g cucumber	£0.15
6 mint leaves	£0.10
20g kale	£0.05
150ml apple juice	£0.15
20ml agave syrup	£0.20
30ml lime juice	£0.18
Garnish	£0.18
Total:	£1.47

EQUIPMENT:
Scales
Blender

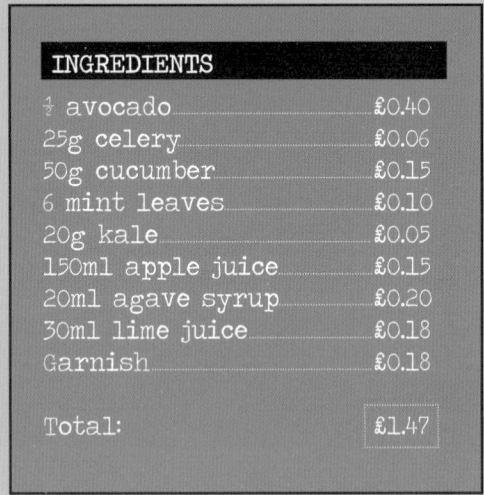

METHOD:
Blend all ingredients with two ice cubes for 30 seconds.

SERVED IN:
Eco-friendly water bottle

ICE:
None

GARNISH:
Kale
Apple
Cucumber

JJ SAYS The juice diet phenomenon has swept the planet, and my world has opened to some incredible new flavours. Remember to shake as you go to stop a pile up of sediment at the bottom of your cup. This is a drink best served cold for flavour so add ice if you need to. You can pre-prep at night, ready for the sprint to work in the morning.

Health benefits:

It's no secret kale is a kick-ass superfood! It's packed with Superman-like antioxidant powers that your body will very much thank you for. In addition, it's high in iron and vitamin K and is great for reducing inflammation within the body. Avocado is no slouch either, hitting you with vitamin E, B6, and folic acid, meaning cholesterol takes a back seat. In your face cholesterol!

DEFIBRILLATOR

I've packed it with everything you need to get your blood pressure back in check each morning with a breakfast drink made from berries, bananas and grains. This creamy yet sour concoction will have no problem sliding down faster than any granola bowl.

INGREDIENTS	
10g muesli	£0.04
100g Black Forest purée*	£0.40
200g Actimel	£0.63
50ml coconut water	£0.18
20ml runny honey	£0.16
1 banana	£0.18
Garnish	£0.09
Total:	£1.68

★ Black Forest purée: Add 600g of frozen Black Forest or summer fruits to 300ml of sugar syrup and blend carefully.

EQUIPMENT:
Scales
Blender

METHOD:
Blend all ingredients with four ice cubes for 30 seconds.

SERVED IN:
Gin balloon glass

ICE:
None

GARNISH:
½ strawberry
1 blueberry
1 blackberry
1 raspberry
1 red seedless grape

 **JJ SAYS**

If you didn't guess by the title I'll tell you now, this drink is aimed at the heart and circulatory system to get you jump-started again! Loads of friendly bacteria are slipped in too, mainly for taste, but it doesn't hurt to know that your digestive system is being looked after as well.

Health benefits:

Berries, in particular blueberries and raspberries are amazing for their antioxidant components, meaning any "free radicals" will be kept in check. Free radicals are responsible for aging, tissue damage, and possibly some diseases. Actimel is a probiotic yoghurt. Probiotics are live bacteria and are believed to help balance the friendly bacteria living in your digestive system.

THE MED

Grapefruit isn't everyone's cup of tea, so I've added oodles of fresh fruit, a drizzle of honey and a hint of cinnamon to capture sunshine in a glass that will make you feel as sexy as the Mediterranean itself.

INGREDIENTS

50g green grapes	£0.20
1 pinch cinnamon powder	£0.01
50g orange flesh	£0.15
50g grapefruit flesh	£0.20
50g tinned peach purée*	£0.09
20ml lemon	£0.12
20ml runny honey	£0.16
50ml tonic water	£0.20
Garnish	£0.03
Total:	**£1.16**

★ Tinned peach purée: Blend one 410g tin of tinned peaches (including syrup), pour into an empty bottle or kilner jar and store in the fridge (lasts up to 2 weeks).

EQUIPMENT:
Scales
Blender

METHOD:
Blend first seven ingredients with four ice cubes for 30 seconds and top with tonic.

SERVED IN:
Gin balloon glass

ICE:
None

GARNISH:
Orange wheel

 **SAYS**

I generally regret ordering the Mediterranean breakfast over the classic British fry-up, but not here. You'll get everything you need on a hot summer's day without the bloated tummy. This will set you up perfectly for chilling out by the pool, reading a good book, all while soaking in the sun from overhead, heaven.

Health benefits:

Superfruits do not get much better than grapefruits. First off, they contain flavonoids, which have been shown to exhibit anti-inflammatory, anti-diabetic, anti-cancer, and neuroprotective activity. They also contain an antioxidant called lycopene which is what gives grapefruit its beautiful 'pink' hue.

CLUB TROPICANA

Wake you up before you go go! Club Tropicana is more than just a hit song by Wham! - it's an easy to make party drink. It normally features light rum, mango and pineapple juice. Our healthy version trades the rum for coconut water so the fun can carry you on through the day.

INGREDIENTS

227g tinned pineapple	£0.50
100g natural yoghurt	£0.20
50ml coconut water	£0.18
5g ginger root	£0.14
100ml fresh mango flesh	£0.70
20ml runny honey	£0.16
20ml lemon	£0.12
Garnish	£0.08
Total:	£2.08

EQUIPMENT:
Scales
Blender

METHOD:
Blend all ingredients with four ice cubes for 30 seconds.

SERVED IN:
Hurricane glass

ICE:
None

GARNISH:
Tinned pineapple slice

 **JL SAYS**

You'll be limbo-dancing for Britain after all that vitamin C. The drink has a good kick and a delicious aftertaste from the sweet and sour combination of pineapple and mango. Though health drinks are often a bit flat, this one will wake you up as well as slide down smoothly.

Health benefits:

This drink is jam-packed with vitamin C thanks to the mango, pineapple and lemon. Vitamin C is crucial for fighting off the common cold and keeping your eyes, gums, bones, skin and blood vessels in tip-top shape. But probably its biggest attribute is its cancer prevention ability! The antioxidant properties of vitamin C protect cells and their DNA from damage and mutation.

IRON MAN

This creamy delight is packed with protein - cashew nuts, almond milk, peanut butter and your gym bunny protein powder so you should have no problem loading the right carbs in to your system and help buff you up after those heavy weight sessions.

INGREDIENTS

20g cashew nuts	£0.04
20g almonds	£0.23
2 bananas	£0.36
50g whey protein powder	£0.60
150ml almond milk	£0.26
30ml runny honey	£0.25
20g peanut butter	£0.08
10ml lemon juice	£0.06
Total:	**£1.88**

EQUIPMENT:
Scales
Blender

METHOD:
Blend all ingredients with four ice cubes for one minute

SERVED IN:
Protein shaker

ICE:
None

GARNISH:
With an arm flex

This tastes far better than your post-gym protein workout fuel! You might need to give it two spins in the blender, though, to make sure the nuts are really broken down and blended in. I've never been a hardcore gym bunny, but some of my hardcore crew consulted on this one to make sure the purists get their protein and I give the flavour they need to get the job done in style.

Health benefits:

Protein intake is a crucial component of your diet. Your muscles need protein to function properly and recover from strenuous exercise. The most effective protein powder to take after exercise is called WPI (whey protein isolate), it is referred to as a complete protein as it contains all the amino acids needed in your daily diet - go get some!

CRUDITÉS

We've taken all your favourite veggie dipping sticks and whizzed them into a delicious savoury smoothie with a hint of chilli. It's long, refreshing and full of flavour, but watch out for the chilli, it's easier to add than to take away when mixing drinks!

INGREDIENTS

100g carrot	£0.04
50g celery	£0.07
50g cucumber	£0.06
A little chopped chilli	£0.02
50g red pepper	£0.21
5g coriander	£0.12
100ml spring water	£0.10
20ml runny honey	£0.16
20ml lime juice	£0.12
Garnish	£0.10
Total:	**£1.00**

EQUIPMENT:
Scales
Blender
Large sieve

METHOD:
Blend all ingredients with three ice cubes for 1 minute, then strain through a sieve into a kilner jar.

SERVED IN:
Kilner jar

ICE:
None

GARNISH:
1 slice bell pepper
½ carrot
1 celery stick
Slice of cucumber

SAYS
Though I love my vegetables, I didn't always. I was shocked when I first tried juices from raw carrot, celery and cucumber as they were almost nothing like the raw vegetables I once despised. So if you're worried that this drink isn't for you, I do recommend blitzing and trying a few out, you may go on to love them as much as I have.

Health benefits:

Another butt-kicking source of antioxidants, carrots are rich in vitamin C, vitamin K, vitamin B8, pantothenic acid, folate, potassium, iron, copper, and manganese. They also pack a ton of vitamin A, which is believed to improve night vision, so if your lifestyle is becoming increasingly similar to that of a vampire, throw a few of these back before the day is out.

ICED GREEN TEA

I don't think there's anything more refreshing than an iced tea straight from the fridge. We all need to have our two litres a day of water, but that can be so boring at times. This drink means you not only get your H_2O packed with flavour, but it's also loaded with minerals that will cleanse your soul.

INGREDIENTS (SERVES 4)	
45ml agave syrup	£0.45
3 green tea bags	£0.24
2 broken lemongrass sticks	£0.70
A little chopped chilli	£0.06
6g ginger	£0.05
900ml spring water	£0.90
Juice of 1 lemon	£0.30
Garnish	£0.02
Total:	£2.72

EQUIPMENT:
Scales
Saucepan
Kilner Jar

METHOD:
Add all the ingredients to a saucepan, bring it to the boil for 2 minutes and then let it sit on the side until its cooled. Pour into a kilner jar and store in the fridge (lasts up to 1 week).

SERVED IN:
Glass tea mug

ICE:
None

GARNISH:
Mint sprig

 It's one of my besties, Sarah Willingham, that got me onto iced green teas, she swears by them. In my line of work "down time" is hard to come across but I'll happily travel the world to have my soul cleansed by her and get my head screwed back on straight. After a therapeutic day out catching up together, iced tea will be the first thing out of her fridge, followed by the wine of course!

Health benefits:

With its origins in China, green tea has been used as a medicine for thousands of years. After being the unsung hero for many years its popularity has risen dramatically due to its many health benefits in comparison to the traditional black tea we drink in good old England. With a higher content of antioxidants, polyphenols which improve brain function and the ability to burn fat, this is some cup of joe!

COLD BREW COFFEE

When we want a coffee, why boil it first? Cold-brewing, or Toddy brewing, is the answer. The flavour you get will be rich and yet floral thanks in part to the lack of heat that makes coffee acidic, meaning there's no need to bump and grind with cold brew!

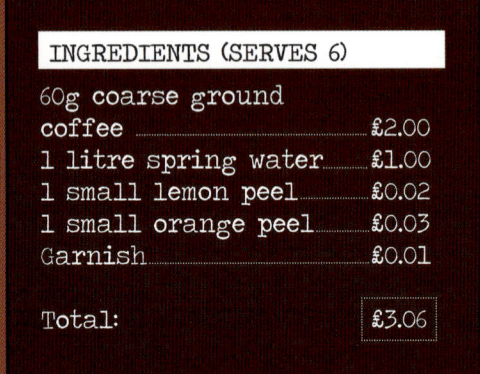

INGREDIENTS (SERVES 6)	
60g coarse ground coffee	£2.00
1 litre spring water	£1.00
1 small lemon peel	£0.02
1 small orange peel	£0.03
Garnish	£0.01
Total:	£3.06

EQUIPMENT:
Scales
Kilner jar

METHOD:
Add all ingredients to a kilner jar, give it a shake for 10 seconds, then keep the jar sealed for 18 hours. Strain through a muslin cloth, bottle, and store in the fridge (lasts up to 1 week).

SERVED IN:
Rocks glass

ICE:
None

GARNISH:
Coffee beans

I don't know why but I've never been able to stomach hot drinks. I've got friends who will happily drink lava, but I have to leave my coffee down to chill, then normally forget about it till it's too late! I love that I can prepare my coffee days in advance, so you don't have to wait for it to cool, let alone boil, before I'm ready to dive in!

Health benefits:

To brew or not to brew, that is the question? Well research now shows the many benefits of cold brewed coffee compared to its heated counterpart. Most notably the increased amounts of antioxidants, this is due to the coffee not being exposed to high temperatures and the fact chlorogenic acid (a type of antioxidant) is very sensitive to heat. Also expect no acid reflux, less acid overall in the coffee and a lower caffeine content which means you can drink until your heart's content.

"Nothing completes Christmas like poorly-packed pressies under a wonky tree. The remains of a cremated turkey carcass sat on the side. The sound of belt buckles breaking from one too many Brussel sprouts, from the extra mouthful you just didn't need. It's time to put your PJs on, snuggle in front of the TV and knock back a winter warmer. From your crazy uncle to your tipsy nan, I've created a cocktail for everyone."

WINTER WARMERS

STICKY TOFFEE
OLD FASHIONED

It always cheers me up to see my favourite dessert, the sticky toffee pudding, mixed in with my favourite whisky cocktail, the Old Fashioned. If the turkey needs a hand washing itself down, reach for one of these to help your digestion along nicely.

INGREDIENTS	
60ml Jack Daniels	£1.20
10ml Werther's Original syrup*	£0.10
1 dash Angostura bitters	£0.05
1 drop vanilla extract	£0.02
Total:	£1.37

★ Werther's Original syrup: In a saucepan add 1 x 50g packet of Werther's Original for every 100ml of sugar syrup (You may also use Sugar Free Werther's Original to make this syrup). Simmer on a medium heat for 6 minutes. Let the mixture cool, pour into an empty bottle or kilner jar and refrigerate (lasts up to 6 weeks).

Original Recipe:

OLD FASHIONED

★ 60ml bourbon
★ 1 white sugar cube
★ 2 dashes Angostura bitters

Add the sugar cube to a rocks/old fashioned glass, saturate with bitters and add a very small splash of water, muddle the sugar cube until dissolved. Fill the glass halfway with cubed ice, add the bourbon and stir for 20 seconds, top up with cubed ice and stir for 10 seconds. Garnish with an orange twist.

EQUIPMENT:
Scales
Mixing spoon
Mixing glass

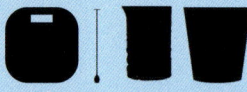

METHOD:
Stir. Add the ingredients to mixing glass filled with cubed ice, stir and strain into rocks glass filled with cubed ice.

SERVED IN:
Rocks glass

ICE:
Cubed ice

GARNISH:
None

 **JC SAYS**

I really do love an Old Fashioned a LOT. The sweetener is usually sugar soaked in Angostura bitters, but you can use almost anything from honey, treacle or molasses, or if you fancy testing your skills, microwave equal parts Werthers Originals to water and use the syrup that it makes, you really can't get this drink wrong.

History:

It was at the Pendennis Club, which is a gentlemen's club in Louisville, Kentucky, when the first use of the name "Old Fashioned" for a Bourbon whiskey cocktail (bourbon whiskey mixed with rock candy syrup and bitters), was used. The recipe is believed to have been invented by a bartender at the club in honour of Colonel James E. Pepper, an influential Bourbon distiller. In 2015 the city of Louisville named the Old Fashioned as its official cocktail. Sounds like our kind of city!

MINCE PIE FLIP

Imagine a Christmas version of Baileys Irish cream, well…. This quick homemade egg nog tastes just that. This is for those of you who love a bit of booze with your festive mince pies. I'm sure if you left one out for Santa he'd take you off the naughty list!

INGREDIENTS	
30ml Scotch whisky	£0.60
2 tsp fruit mincemeat	£0.05
1 whole egg	£0.15
20ml cream	£0.08
5ml vanilla extract	£0.10
10ml sugar syrup	£0.01
Garnish	£0.06
Total:	£1.05

EQUIPMENT:
Scales
Spoon
Cocktail shaker
Hawthorne strainer
Fine strainer

METHOD:
Shake. Add all ingredients to your shaker, add cubed ice, shake and fine strain into a chilled coupe glass.

SERVED IN:
Coupe glass

ICE:
None

GARNISH:
Orange twist

I love flips of all styles, but this one is the king! Fruit "mince" (I always imagine minced meat for some reason) is available year round and it's packed with flavour from orange, cinnamon, ginger and nutmeg to sultanas and raisins. I love this cocktail by itself, but feel free to pour it over your Christmas cake, you'll never go back to regular cream again!

Original Recipe:

SNOWBALL

★ 50ml Warninks Advocaat
★ 150ml lemonade
★ Juice of 1 lime wedge

Add the Advocaat and lime juice to a tall glass filled with ice, top with lemonade and gently stir. Garnish with an orange wheel.

History:

The Snowball is thought to have originated in Britain in the late 1940s or early 1950s. The key ingredient in a snowball is Advocaat, a Dutch liqueur made traditionally from egg, sugar and brandy. Advocaat translates to "lawyer" in Dutch, due to the belief that the liqueur soothed the throat, making it ideal for public speaking, especially in the courtroom! Warninks is the world's oldest manufacturer of Advocaat, originating in 1616, who use a staggering 60 million eggs a year!

BLUE BLAZER

This flaming brandy cocktail laden with festive spices knocks lighting the Christmas pud on fire to shame. Or even better, use it to flame your pudding! Either way, sipping this great classic cocktail, the smell of logs burning, slumped on the sofa with your slippers on, will certainly be a fuzzy feeling you won't regret.

INGREDIENTS

100ml brandy	£2.00
Peel of 1 orange and 1 lemon	£0.18
Pinch cinnamon	£0.01
1 star anise	£0.07
2 raisins	£0.01
2 pieces dried apricot	£0.20
1 tsp brown sugar	£0.01
Garnish	£0.06
Total:	**£2.54**

EQUIPMENT:
Scales
Spoon
Blow torch

METHOD:
Build. Warm a brandy snifter with hot water then discard. Add all the ingredients into the warm glass and set alight with blow torch, letting it burn for 10 seconds before blowing out.

SERVED IN:
Brandy snifter

ICE:
None

GARNISH:
Orange twist

Traditionally this mix is made by passing between two small saucepans. If you've already had a few on Christmas Day then you might NOT want to try this at home. But if you fancy giving it a spin, maybe do it over the sink, and watch out for red hot glass rims, you don't want to burn your lips and end up looking like a real joker.

Original Recipe:

BLU BLAZER

★ 60ml Scotch whisky
★ 60ml boiling water
★ 1 tbsp powdered sugar

Using two metal mugs, add the boiling water and whisky to one mug and quickly ignite. Carefully throw the ignited liquid between the two mugs increasing the distance with each throw. Serve in a brandy snifter with a lemon twist for garnish.
BE VERY CAREFUL, PRACTICE WITH WATER BEFOREHAND!

History:

The Blue Blazer was created by the legendary Jerry "The Professor" Thomas while he was barman at the El Dorado in San Francisco in the late 1800s. Jerry, who is considered a god in the bartending fraternity, was a star performer with this drink. He created and perfected the technique of lighting whisky and throwing the flaming liquid between two silver tankards. An impressive manoeuvre that is believed to be the world's first 'flair bartending move'.

TERRY'S CHOCOLATE MULLED WINE

Nothing screams Christmas like the smell of mulled wine in the air and I can't get enough of this recipe! Not even a full-blooded Scrooge could resist at least a glass on a frosty Christmas Day, so lock the doors, switch on the fire, and let this classic warm your soul!

INGREDIENTS

Ingredient	Price
100ml Scotch whisky	£2.14
750ml shiraz red wine	£7.50
1 (157g) Terry's Chocolate Orange	£2.00
10 cloves	£0.10
5 star anise	£0.40
2 cinnamon sticks	£0.60
1g powdered nutmeg	£0.05
75g brown sugar	£0.21
Juice of 1 orange & rind	£0.30
Garnish	£0.10
Total:	**£13.40**

(£2.68 per person)

EQUIPMENT:
Scales
Saucepan
Wooden spoon

METHOD:
Stir. Add all ingredients into a large saucepan, simmer for 6-8 minutes until all the chocolate has dissolved. Remove from heat, leave to stand for 5 minutes then pour from saucepan to mugs.

SERVED IN:
Poured from the saucepan into your favourite mug

ICE:
None

GARNISH:
1 star anise
1 half of an orange slice
Grated nutmeg

Original Recipe:

TRADITIONAL ENGLISH MULLED WINE

★ 1 bottle cheap red wine
★ 60ml brandy ★ 60ml orange juice
★ 40ml lemon juice
★ 50g demerara sugar
★ 2 star anise
★ 2 pinches grated nutmeg
★ 2 pinches cinnamon
★ 1 pinch powdered ginger
★ 1 vanilla pod

Gently heat the ingredients in a saucepan before dispensing into toddy glasses. Garnish with an orange slice studded with some cloves.

 **JL SAYS:** The Terry's Chocolate Orange always comes out at Christmas yet never seems to get finished at my house. Whether you're a fan or not, I've found a perfect way to knock it back that will have you queuing up for more. Change or take the chocolate out if you like, it'll still taste divine!

History:

Originating in the 2nd century, it was created by the Romans who would heat wine to defend their bodies during winter. The word 'mulled' simply means heated and spiced. Traditionally in England it's red wine, but it's not uncommon to see mead (honey wine) or cider being mulled. Oh… Christmas how we miss you!

IRISH COFFEE

When winter comes flooding in you can keep your Guinness, I like to get my "moustache" from an Irish coffee! This classic Irish brew will pick you up and get you going. Sipping through cold cream in to hot coffee is a flavour explosion we should never forget.

INGREDIENTS	
50ml Irish whiskey	£1.60
50ml double cream	£0.17
75ml black coffee (hot)	£0.10
1 tsp brown sugar	£0.01
Pinch of powdered nutmeg	£0.01
Garnish	£0.01
Total:	£1.90

EQUIPMENT:
Scales
Kettle
Mixing spoon
Cocktail shaker
Hawthorne strainer

METHOD:
Build. Add the hot coffee, whiskey, sugar, and nutmeg to the glass first, give it a good stir to dissolve the sugar. In your shaker add the double cream with five ice cubes, shake and gently layer on top of the coffee in the glass.

SERVED IN:
Irish coffee glass

ICE:
None

GARNISH:
Grated nutmeg

JJ SAYS

I can't emphasise enough how satisfying taking your first sip of an Irish coffee can be. Two of my favourite bars in the world do it better than most. So if you're in London, head down to Swift in Soho, or if you find yourself State-side make sure you stop in at The Dead Rabbit in New York to test your home creations against the best there is.

Original Recipe:

IRISH COFFEE

★ 50ml Irish whiskey
★ 100ml hot coffee
★ 2 tbsp brown sugar
★ 50ml double cream

Add the whiskey, coffee and sugar into a toddy glass and stir until sugar is dissolved. Slightly whip the cream and carefully float on top. No garnish originally, but fresh nutmeg can be grated on top.

IRISH COFFEE (Joe's Original Recipe):
Cream - Rich as an Irish Brogue
Coffee - Strong as a Friendly Hand
Sugar - Sweet as the tongue of a Rogue
Whiskey - Smooth as the Wit of the Land

History:

The Irish Coffee is the brainchild of Joe Sheridan, an Irish chef working at the flying boat terminal of Foynes airport near Shannon. During a wintery night in 1942 a flight bound for New York had to be turned back due to bad weather. Joe decided to prepare something a little special for the returning passengers to warm them up. Legend has it there was a hushed silence as the passengers drank his warm brew for the first time. "Hey buddy," said a surprised American passenger, "is this Brazilian coffee?" "No," said Joe, that's an Irish Coffee." The drink was a huge success, so much so that in 1952 Joe was asked to move to San Francisco to make his famous coffee at the Buena Vista Hotel. Joe accepted!

COCO POP LATTE

This sweet latte coffee is enriched with Baileys and chocolate sauce - and a liberal helping of snap, crackle and pop! Everyone loves a hot chocolate, but this time it comes with a gentle kick to push you through on a cold winter's night.

INGREDIENTS

50ml Baileys	£1.07
25g Coco Pops	£0.10
150ml whole milk	£0.06
½ tsp instant coffee	£0.04
5ml sugar syrup*	£0.01
15ml chocolate sauce	£0.18
Garnish	£0.08
Total:	**£1.54**

★ In a saucepan add 500ml caster sugar to 500ml of hot water from the kettle, gently simmer until all the sugar has dissolved and the syrup is clear. Let it cool, then pour into an empty bottle and refrigerate (lasts up to 6 weeks).

EQUIPMENT:
Scales
Cocktail shaker
Hawthorne strainer
Fine strainer

METHOD:
Shake. Add all the ingredients to your shaker, add cubed ice, shake and fine strain into a chilled mini milk bottle.

SERVED IN:
Mini (250ml) milk bottle

ICE:
None

GARNISH:
Squirty cream
Chocolate sauce
Small handful of Coco Pops

SAYS

Coco Pops were my favourite breakfast treat growing up, and as I've got older it's dwindled to a rather depressing coffee and a cigarette. The little bit of chocolate milk at the bottom of my bowl was always the best bit, so this drink is dedicated to just that. "Cereal milk infusions" are great fun, so if you're up for a twist, heat any classic cereal with milk, and sip away. Crunchy Nut Cornflakes and white chocolate is a close second!

Original Recipe:

CAFFE MOCHA

★ 1 espresso shot
★ 20ml dark chocolate sauce
★ 120ml hot milk

Build and stir and serve in a latte glass with a dusting of chocolate powder.

History:

What is now called a latte in English-speaking countries is shorthand for the Italian "Caffelatte" or "milk coffee", though in northern Europe and Scandinavia you'll need to call for a "Café au lait" if you'd like this soothing hot drink. Be careful when to order one in its home country Italy; lattes are for breakfast and should never be drunk after midday!

HOT TODDY

This drink is guaranteed to warm the cockles of your heart while putting hairs on your chest! Whisky, infused with star anise, cloves, cinnamon, honey and lemon... what's not to love?! Be sure to fill up a flask before you pop your wellies on for those long winter walks.

INGREDIENTS (SERVES 4)	
250ml Scotch whisky	£5.00
100ml runny honey	£0.80
¼ lemon	£0.30
2 sticks cinnamon	£0.60
8 cloves	£0.08
4 star anise	£0.32
250ml apple juice	£0.25
Total:	**£7.35**
	(£1.83 per person)

EQUIPMENT:
Saucepan
Wooden spoon
Thermos

METHOD:
Add all the ingredients to saucepan, simmer for 4-5 minutes then pour straight into Thermos flask.

SERVED IN:
Thermos flask

ICE:
None

GARNISH:
None

JJ SAYS

Growing up my mom would make me one when I got a cold, as her mother would have done for her. I hated the taste then, but now that's fully changed I can see a few away with ease. For all the winter warmers I love, this one seems to be the first choice to take for a walk, whether you've gone sledging, or even just building a snowman, this little beauty will keep you ticking over.

Original Recipe:

HOT TODDY

★ 60ml Scotch whisky
★ 20ml lemon juice
★ 15ml honey
★ 15ml sugar syrup
★ 4 cloves
★ 75ml boiling water

Stir and serve in a toddy glass with a cinnamon stick for garnish.

History:

The 'Hot Toddy' originated in India during the 1700s from a drink produced by fermenting the sap of palm trees, specifically the toddy palm, hence the name. The British, who have always been fond of taking things that aren't theirs, nicked the idea and claimed it as their own. Though the Irish dispute this. They say an Irish doctor named Robert Bentley Todd used to tell his patients to drink hot brandy, cinnamon, and sugar water.

PERFECT CUP OF TEA

This next drink is bound to be the most controversial in this book but you can't not start the day with the perfect cup of tea! I've had more bad ones than good, so here we are setting the record straight with debatably the most important drink on the planet. After years of trying to master the correct 'dunk', I've even thrown in my top three biscuits to have with your perfect cuppa!

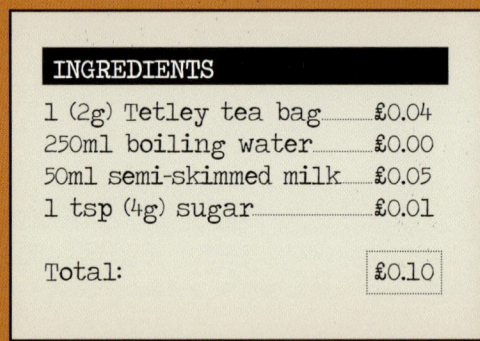

INGREDIENTS	
1 (2g) Tetley tea bag	£0.04
250ml boiling water	£0.00
50ml semi-skimmed milk	£0.05
1 tsp (4g) sugar	£0.01
Total:	£0.10

EQUIPMENT:
Scales
Teaspoon
Kettle

METHOD:
Boil the kettle. Add tea bag to the mug, then add 250ml of boiling water. Allow the tea bag to steep for 4 minutes, occasionally giving it a stir. Press the tea bag against the side of the mug before removing to ensure full flavour, discard tea bag to bin (not the sink, we're not animals), add 50ml of semi-skimmed milk and stir to combine. Finally add one level (4g) spoon of caster sugar and stir. Sit back and relax!

SERVED IN:
LCC mug

Did you know?

165 million cups of tea are consumed a day in the UK alone! Though the first advert for tea in England appeared in a publication in 1658, describing it simply as a "China Drink," but by the mid-18th century tea had become Britain's most popular beverage, replacing ale and gin as the drink of the masses. It wasn't long until the likes of the East India Company were using fast ships called tea clippers to bring back leaves from India and China. The only surviving clipper of its kind, the 'Cutty Sark,' can still be visited in Greenwich after being damaged by a fire in 2007.

To many this isn't quite a "cocktail", but to a man who sometimes blends aftershaves in a morning, everything is a cocktail! The cup of tea has been a part of my life since birth, so getting one perfect seems like the perfect way to finish this book! Please remember… Adding more than two sugars means it's not a cup of tea it's a milkshake!

JJ'S TOP 3 DUNKING BISCUITS:

★ Shortbread (11 sec recommended dunking time)
★ Chocolate Hobnob (5 sec recommended dunking time)
★ Custard cream (8 sec recommended dunking time)

There is nothing worse than a soggy biscuit in the bottom of your brew. Take into consideration my recommended dunk times to avoid embarrassment in front of your fellow tea drinking aficionados.

RAYMOND BLANC'S CHEESE FONDUE

"This simple recipe is a real crowd-pleaser after a big night out. It is a sociable dish which draws everyone around the table to watch the delicious fondue bubble while they dip their crusty pieces of bread into it. In my home of Franche-Comté, this dish is the heart and soul of a beautiful evening shared with friends… alongside a little glass of Kirsch, bien sûr." *Raymond Blanc OBE*

Serves: 4
Preparation time: 5 minutes
Cooking time: 10 minutes
Special equipment: Fondue set

INGREDIENTS:
1 clove of garlic cut in half
300ml white wine, dry
300g Comté cheese, small dice
300g Gruyère cheese, small dice
3 tsp cornflour
3 tbsp Kirsch
Freshly ground black pepper
1 baguette cut into bite-sized pieces

METHOD:
In a medium-sized fondue pot, rub the inside with the cut side of the garlic clove and discard.
Place the pot on full heat, add the wine and bring to a boil for 30 seconds (*1).
Turn down to a low heat and add the cheese, stirring until the cheese melts.
Mix together the cornflour and Kirsch, then add it to the cheese. Cook for 2-3 minutes, stirring constantly, until thick and creamy (*2).
Season with a little black pepper to taste and place on the table for your guests.
Spear the bread on fondue forks and dip into the cheese.

CHEF'S NOTES (*):
*1 By bringing the wine to a quick boil you will remove the harsh taste of the alcohol and leave the fruity qualities of the wine.
*2 The fondue should have a smooth, thick-sauce texture. If it is too thin, add more cheese, or stir in a little more cornflour, mixed with Kirsch. If it is too thick, stir in some boiled white wine. The addition of the wine will not only balance the dish with its acidity but also help with the emulsification of the fat in the cheese. If the fondue does split, add a small splash of warm white wine and stir on a medium heat until it has emulsified once again.

VARIATIONS:
Some diced smoked Morteau sausage or large sautéed mushrooms could be skewered with the bread, then dipped.

Recipe © Raymond Blanc 2017

INDEX

A

Absinthe 52
Advocaat 204
Ale 66, 70
All-Day Breakfast Bloody Mary 168
Amaretto 72, 114, 116, 120, 124, 142
Americano 82
Angel Delight Flip 112
Angostura bitters 44, 94, 144
Aperol Spritz 84
Apple & Blackberry Crumble 118
Apple Martini 134

B

B52 142
Bacon & Egg Martini 180
Baileys 112, 116, 120, 122, 124, 142, 212
Banoffee Sundae 114
Bartender's Breakfast 178
Bee's Knees 152
Bellini 58
Beverly Hills Iced Tea 162
Black Velvet 72
Blackcurrant cordial 64, 72, 88, 96
Blackcurrant soufflé 62
Bloody Mary 166
Blow Job 142
Blu Blazer 206
Blue Blazer 206
Boilermakers 66
Bourbon 66, 124, 138, 150, 170, 180, 202
Brain Haemorrhage 142
Bramble 96
Bramley Apple Smash 50
Brandy 50, 108, 206
Brandy Alexander 118
Brandy Crusta 94
Breakfast Martini 176
Breakfast Mimosa 176

Brixton Riot 140
Bull Shot 170
Butter Beer 70

C

Cachaça 42
Caesar 172
Caffe Mocha 212
Caipirinha 42
Calvados 66
Campari 82, 84
Candy Shop Collins 148
Cava 60
Champagne 62, 64, 72, 86, 162, 176
Charlie Sheen 138
Chocolate Hardshake 122
Cider 66, 72
Claret Punch 108
Clover Club 88
Club Tropicana 190
Coca-Cola 72, 162
Coco Pop Latte 212
Coffee 122, 198, 210, 212
Cognac 54, 94, 118
Cointreau 138, 176
Cold Brew Coffee 198
Cookies & Cream 124
Cosmopolitan 136
Cream soda 148
Crème de Cacao 118
Crudités 194
Cuptail 120
Curry Mary 172

D

Daiquiri 46
Dark 'N' Stormy 160
Defibrillator 186
Dirty Banana 114
Doctor Pepper 72

E

Earl Grey Sour 106
Elderflower cordial 50, 60
Elderflower Garden Party 60
Espresso Martini 126
Eton Mess 116

F

Fish House Punch 40

G

Gibson Martini 76
Gin 50, 76, 78, 82, 84, 86, 88, 90, 96, 106, 116, 150, 152, 156, 162, 172, 176
Gin Rickey 150
Ginger ale 100
Grand Marnier 108, 142
Grenadine 44, 72, 142, 144
Guinness (stout) 68, 72
Guinness Punch 68

H

Heisenberg 130
Honey Bee Fizz 152
Hot Buttered Rum 70
Hot Toddy 214
House Bloody Mary 166

I

Iced Green Tea 196
Iced Teas 162
Irish Coffee 210
Irish Milk Punch 68
Iron Man 192

J

Jam Jar Daiquiri 46
JJ's Ultimate All-Day Full English 168
John Collins 156

K

Kahlua 114, 124, 126, 142

L

Lager 66, 72, 158, 174
Lager Shandy 72
Lagerita 158
Lassi 102
Lavender Paloma 80
Lipton ice tea 40
Long Island Iced Tea 162
Long Beach Iced Tea 162

M

Mai Tai 98
Malibu 48
Mango Lassi 102
Maraschino liqueur 94
Margarita 138
Martinez 76
Martini 76, 90, 132, 176, 180
Med, The 188
Medicinal Cordial 100
Michelada 174
Midori 162
Milk 112, 114, 116, 122, 212, 216
Mimosa 176
Mint Julep, The Real (Jerry Thomas) 50
Mince Pie Flip 204
Mintless Mojito 154
Mojito 154
Monaco 72
Moscow Mule 148
Mudslide 122

N

Negroni 82

O

Old Fashioned 202

P

Paloma 80
Peach purée 52, 140, 150
Peach schnapps 52, 142
Perfect Cup of Tea 216
Pimm's 64
Pimm's Cup 64
Pimm's Royal 64
Piña Colada 48
Porn Star Martini 132
Posset 112
Prosecco 58, 80, 132
Punch 40, 44, 108

R

Ramos Gin Fizz 86
Ramos Gin Silver Fizz 86
Raymond Blanc Cheese Fondue 218
Red Eye 174
Red wine 54, 108, 208
Reggae Rum Punch 44
Rose Petal Martini 90
Rose Water Julab 90
Rum 40, 44, 46, 48, 50, 98, 100, 114, 118, 140, 144, 154, 160, 162
Rum punch 44

S

Sambuca 142
Sangria 54
Screaming Orgasm 124
Sex on the Beach 52
Shandy Gaff 72
Sherry 104, 120
Sherry Cobbler 104
Sherry Flip 120
Shooters 142
Shrub 100
Sidecar 94
Silver Gin Fizz 72
Slippery Nipple 142
Smoked Apple Martini 134
Snakebite 72
Snowball 204
Spritzer 60
Sticky Toffee Old Fashioned 202
Stone Fruit Sour 150
Strawberry Shortcake 116
Sunday Roast Bloody Mary 170
Swizzle My Tie 98

T

Tequila 80, 130, 138, 158, 162, 178
Terry's Chocolate Mulled Wine 208
Tia Maria 126
Tokyo Iced Tea 162
Tom Collins 156
Tommy's Margarita 158
Traditional English Mulled Wine 208
Triple Sec 108, 162
Turbo Shandy 72

V

Velvet Falernum 130, 134
Vermouth 76, 82, 88
Victoria's Secret 184
Vodka 42, 52, 112, 114, 122, 126, 132, 134, 136, 148, 162, 166, 168, 170, 172

W

Waterloo Sunset 84
Watermelon Cairpiroska 42
Whisk(e)y 66, 68, 102, 124, 134, 138, 204, 206, 208, 210, 214
Whiskey Sour 180
White Lady 106
White wine 60

Z

Zaza 78
Zombie 144
Zombie Apocalypse 144

JJ'S RECOMMENDED READS

I hope this book has inspired you.
Here are some books that inspired me:

Difford's Guide to Cocktails
Simon Difford

Rum The Manual
Dave Broom

The Joy of Mixology
Gary Regan

The Curious Bartender
Tristan Stephenson

Bon Vivant
Jerry Thomas

Imbibe
David Wondrich

The Craft of the Cocktail
Dale DeGroff

World's Best Cocktails
Tom Sandham

Liquid Intelligence
Dave Arnold

Molecular Gastronomy
Hervé This

J.J. GOODMAN
BARTENDER